1983 EDITION

LEGAL RESEARCH EXERCISES

TO ACCOMPANY

HOW TO FIND THE LAW

(EIGHTH EDITION)

By

Lynn Foster
School of Law Library
Southern Illinois University

and

Elizabeth Slusser Kelly
School of Law Library
Southern Illinois University

St. Paul, Minn.
WEST PUBLISHING CO.
1983

ISBN 0-314-77633-8

ACKNOWLEDGMENTS

There are many people whose support enabled us to make this workbook a reality. First, we thank Morris Cohen, Director of Yale University Law Library, and Bob Berring, Director of the University of California-Berkeley Law Library, who invited us to write the book in conjunction with How to Find the Law.

Second, our thanks go to the two people who alternately coaxed and placated the word processor, Julie Leeper and Vera Felts. Their dedication to this project has gone above and beyond the call of duty.

Three talented and intelligent research assistants, Beth Kamp, Bob White, and Paula Donner Walter, risked their sanity by working through the problems in this workbook. Their comments were extremely helpful.

Two of our colleagues, Ann Puckett and Laurel Wendt, also enriched the quality of the workbook by their comments. We would also like to commend their patience. (No one who writes a problem book ever realizes beforehand how much time it will take.)

Finally, we would like to thank our better halves, Jim Dinkins and Matt Kelly, for their support.

iii

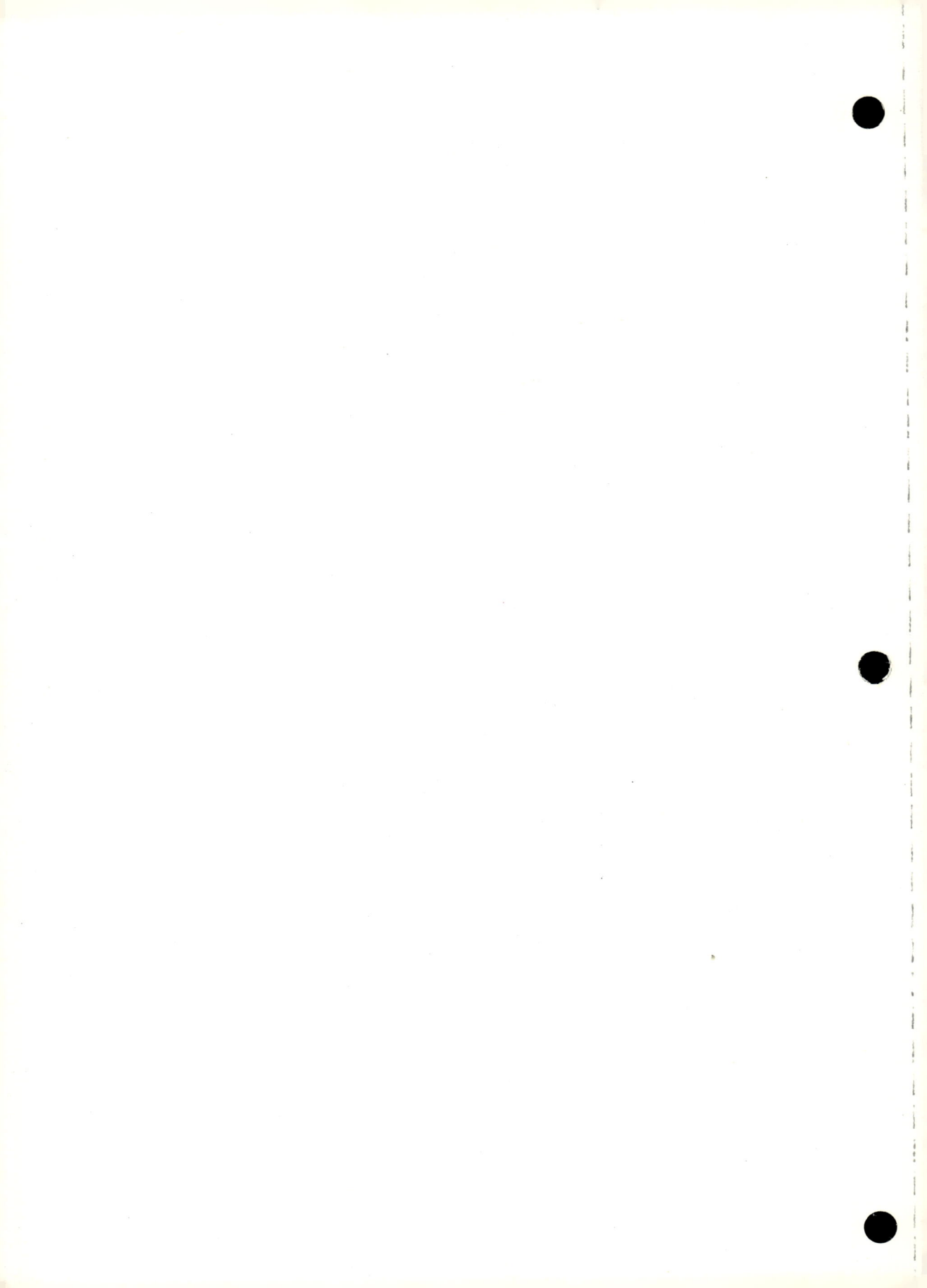

TABLE OF CONTENTS

INTRODUCTION

This workbook was intended to help you learn to do legal research. The ability to perform legal research is a skill which every attorney should have. In the course of completing the assignments in this book, you should:

1) develop a basic familiarity with the kinds of information contained in the research materials in this book and with how to gain access to this information.

2) be able to use this knowledge to formulate basic research strategy.

When you begin a research problem, you will always know certain facts, such as the subject in which you are interested, or the name of a case, or a docket number, etc. The facts you know should determine the legal reference materials that you will use. A good researcher will be able to choose the most appropriate material or materials to use and be able to make the most efficient use of valuable time.

Each chapter in this book is preceded by an introduction which you should read before starting the assignment. Generally, you should also read the appropriate sections of Cohen and Berring, How to Find the Law, 8th ed., before beginning each assignment. You may also be required to read special material such as West's Law Finder, or Lawyers Co-op's The Living Law. Sometimes you will need to use a Uniform System of Citation, 13th ed., in order to provide the correct citation form for one of your answers.

None of the questions in this book are intended to be extremely time-consuming. If you have a problem finding an answer, and have consulted the appropriate text to no avail, ask your instructor for help.

Good luck, and we hope that this workbook will contribute to your effort to become a good lawyer.

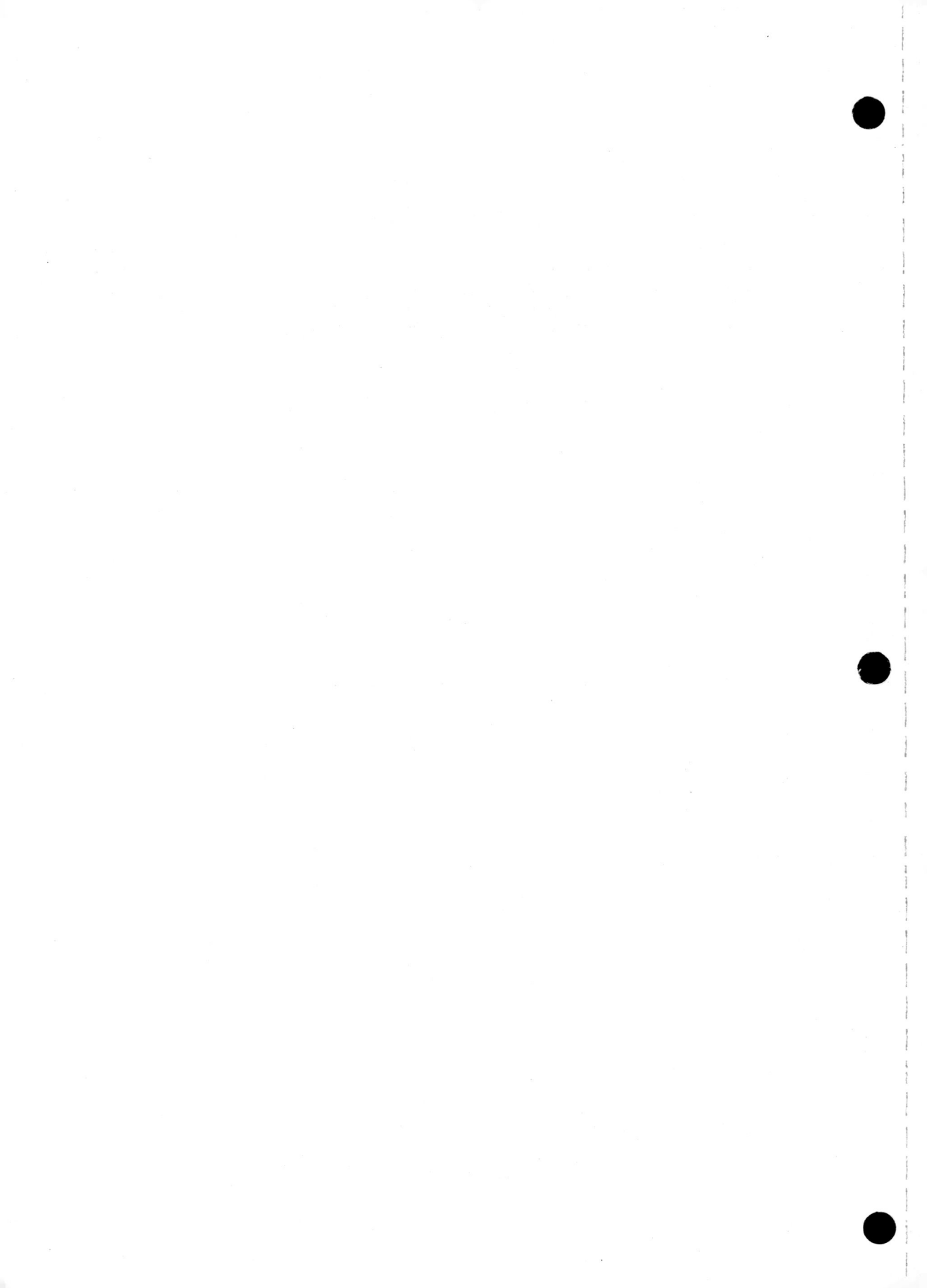

INTRODUCTION
TO CHAPTER I
CASE RETRIEVAL AND CITATION STYLE

The purposes of this assignment are twofold: (1) to give you practice at finding cases for which you have citations and (2) to begin to familiarize you with the rules for citing case names in A Uniform System of Citation, 13th ed. You will need to use A Uniform System, various volumes of the National Reporter System, Federal Cases, and the United States Reports.

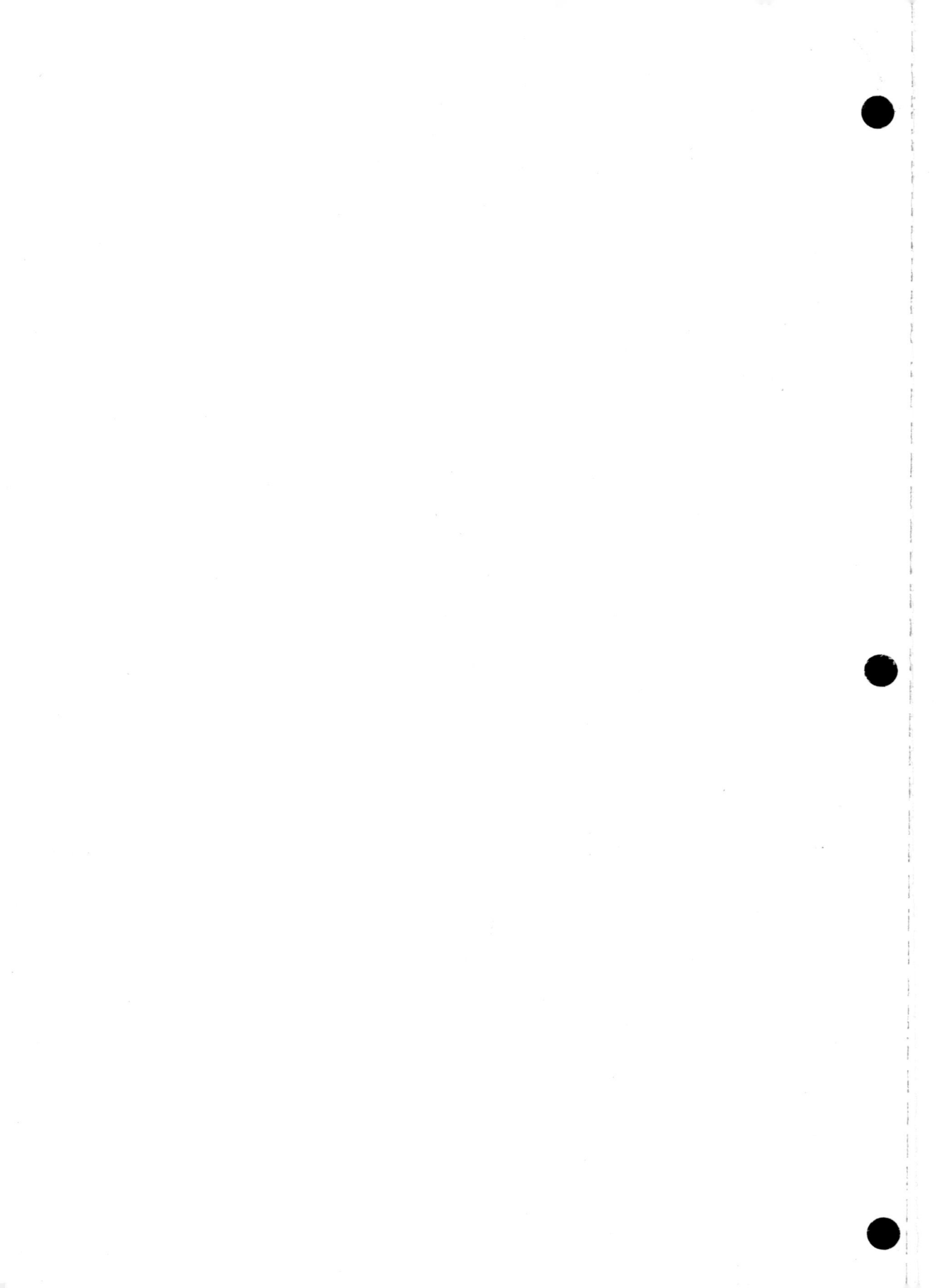

GOALS: 1) To accustom you to finding cases for which you have citations.
          2) To begin to familiarize you with the rules for citing case names
             in A Uniform System of Citation, 13th ed.

Look up each citation in the designated reporter volume. Convert the name or
style of the opinion as it appears on the page indicated to appropriate form
according to A Uniform System of Citation, 13th ed., Rules 1.1, 10.2, and 10.5.
State both the name and year of the opinion, in the format for briefs and
memoranda.

1. 194 A. 318   **ANSWER:**

2. 244 S.E.2d 516   **ANSWER:**

3. 63 N.W. 519   **ANSWER:**

4. 189 P. 690   **ANSWER:**

5. 581 S.W.2d 682   **ANSWER:**

6. 69 Cal. Rptr. 251   **ANSWER:**

7. 6 F.R.D. 475   **ANSWER:**

8. 182 F.2d 712   **ANSWER:**

9. 384 U.S. 436   **ANSWER:**

10. 7 F. Cas. 632   **ANSWER:**

7

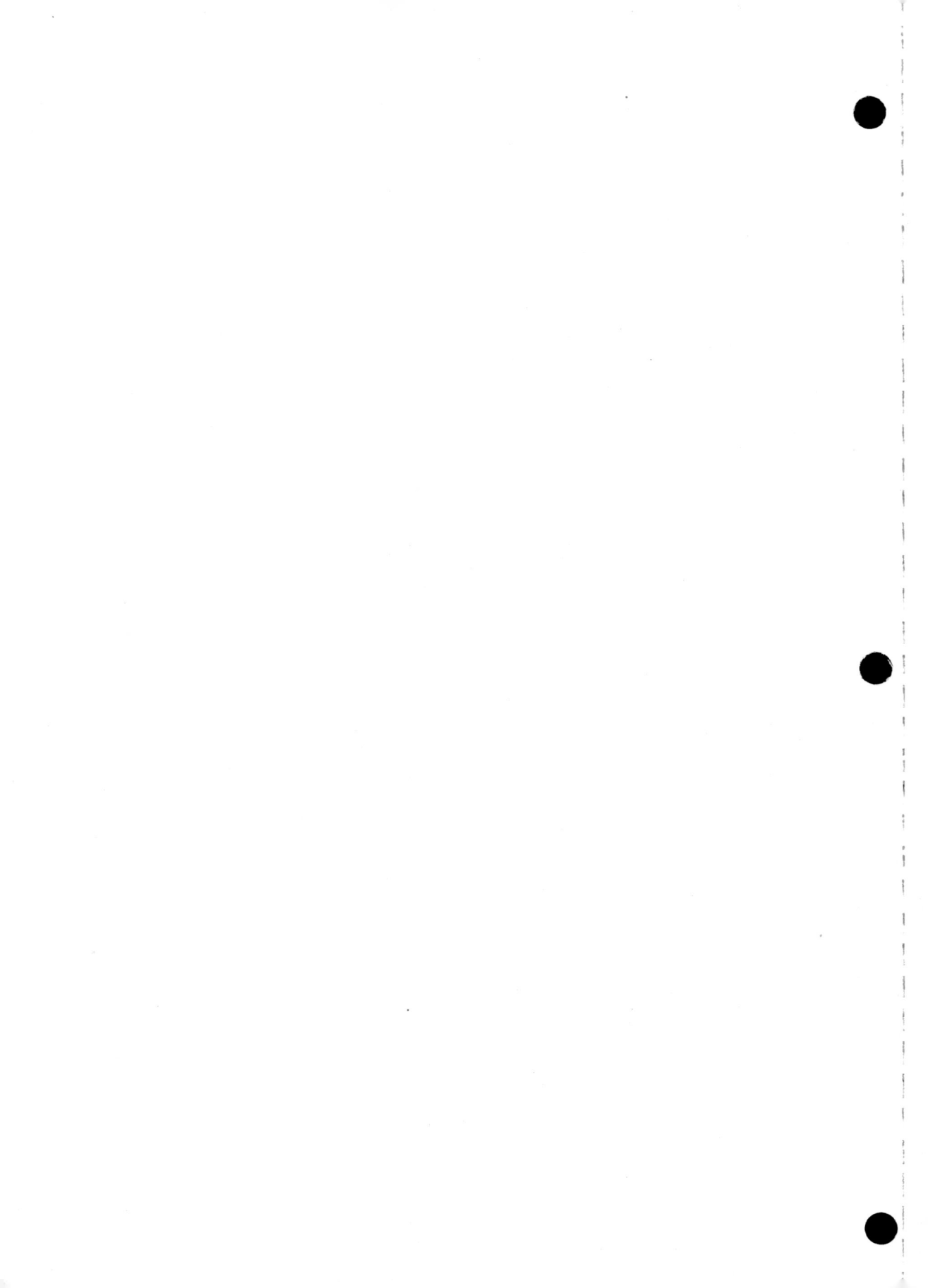

GOALS: 1) To accustom you to finding cases for which you have citations.
2) To begin to familiarize you with the rules for citing case names in A Uniform System of Citation, 13th ed.

Look up each citation in the designated reporter volume. Convert the name or style of the opinion as it appears on the page indicated to appropriate form according to A Uniform System of Citation, 13th ed., Rules 1.1, 10.2, and 10.5. State both the name and year of the opinion, in the format for briefs and memoranda.

    1. 51 S.E. 358   **ANSWER:**

    2. 276 So. 2d 475   **ANSWER:**

    3. 61 N.E.2d 277   **ANSWER:**

    4. 23 N.W.2d 634   **ANSWER:**

    5. 76 P. 891   **ANSWER:**

    6. 283 S.W. 285   **ANSWER:**

    7. 210 N.Y.S. 374   **ANSWER:**

    8. 137 Cal. Rptr. 275   **ANSWER:**

    9. 303 F. Supp. 411   **ANSWER:**

    10. 78 U.S. 616   **ANSWER:**

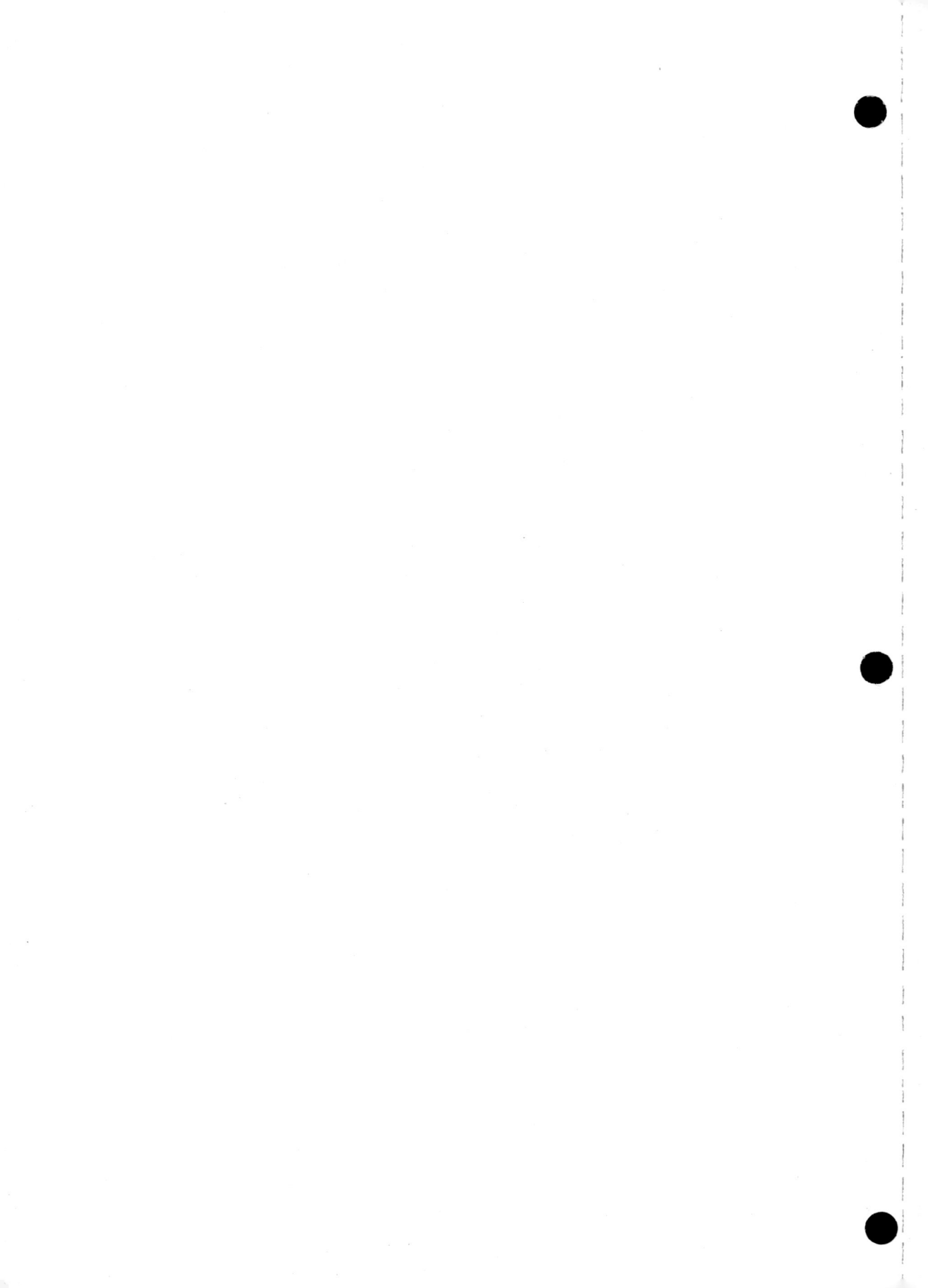

GOALS: 1) To accustom you to finding cases for which you have citations.
2) To begin to familiarize you with the rules for citing case names in
A Uniform System of Citation, 13th ed.

Look up each citation in the designated reporter volume. Convert the name or
style of the opinion as it appears on the page indicated to appropriate form
according to A Uniform System of Citation, 13th ed., Rules 1.1, 10.2, and 10.5.
State both the name and year of the opinion, in the format for briefs and
memoranda.

1. 160 A.2d 265   **ANSWER:**

2. 184 S.E. 452   **ANSWER:**

3. 355 N.E.2d 686   **ANSWER:**

4. 289 N.W.2d 67   **ANSWER:**

5. 125 P.2d 379   **ANSWER:**

6. 187 S.W. 617   **ANSWER:**

7. 46 Cal. Rptr. 278   **ANSWER:**

8. 45 F.R.D. 285   **ANSWER:**

9. 291 F. 253   **ANSWER:**

10. 409 F. Supp. 516   **ANSWER:**

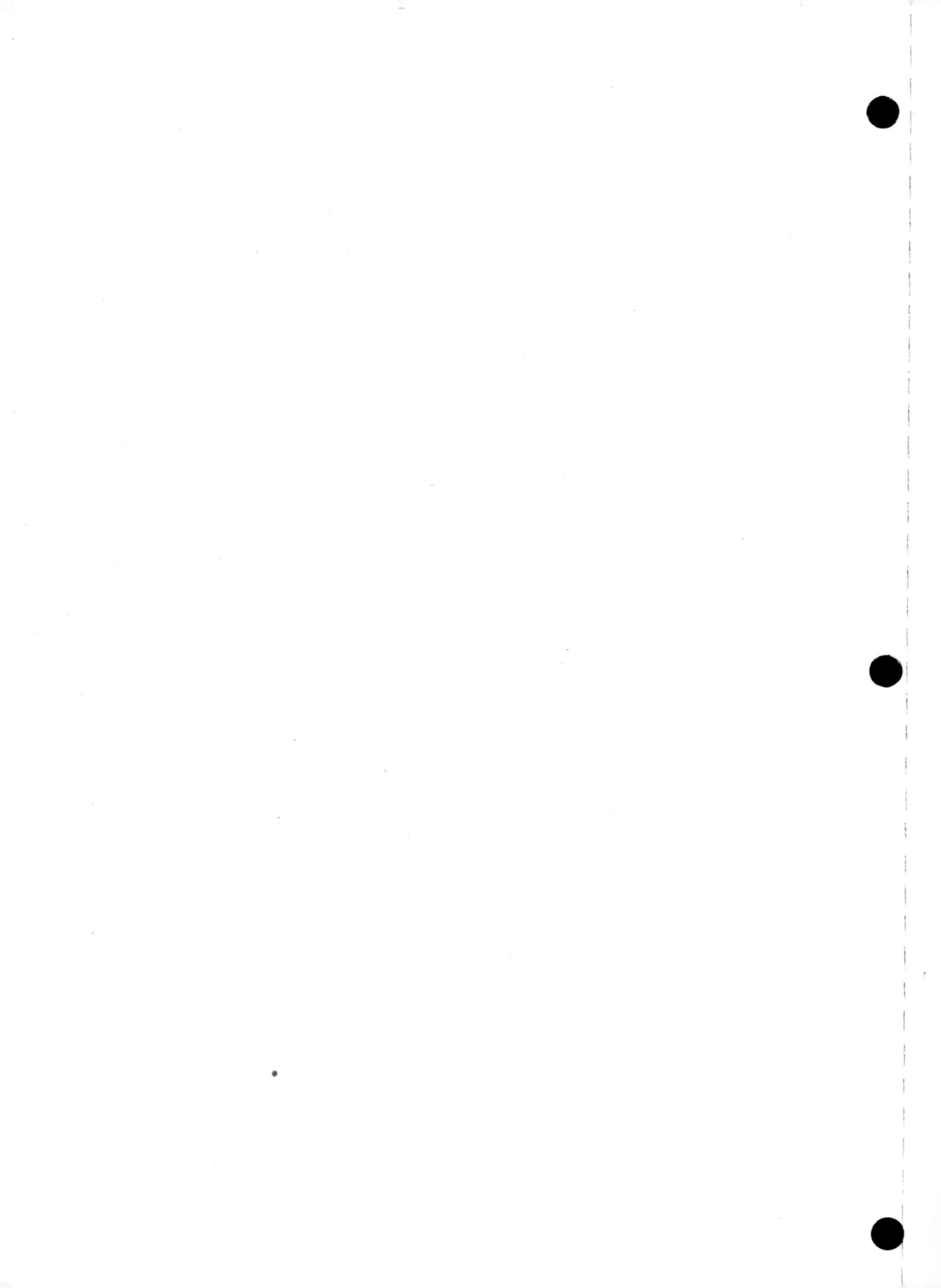

INTRODUCTION
TO CHAPTER II
U.S. SUPREME COURT REPORTERS AND PARTS OF A CASE

This assignment will require you to compare and contrast the three U.S. Supreme Court reporters. The purposes of this assignment are 1) to cause you to learn which kinds of information about a Supreme Court case are available in all the competing reporters, 2) which kinds of information can be found in only one or two of the reporters, and 3) to familiarize you with the parts of a case.

You will use the official United States Reports (U.S.), the unofficial Supreme Court Reporter (S. Ct.), and the unofficial United States Supreme Court Reports--Lawyers' Edition (L. Ed.).

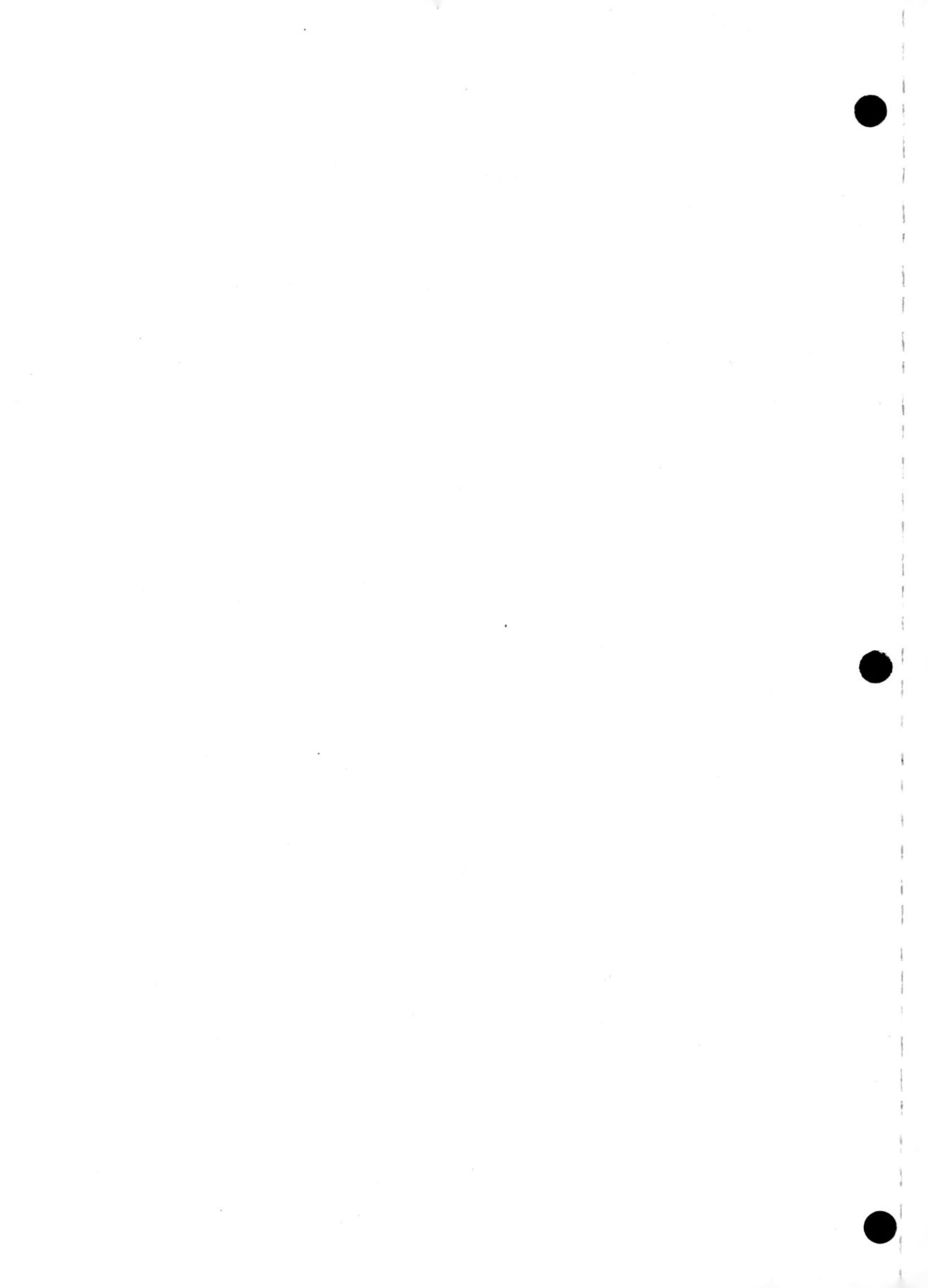

ASSIGNMENT II
U.S. SUPREME COURT REPORTERS AND PARTS OF A CASE
EXERCISE A

GOALS: 1)   To teach you which kinds of information about a Supreme Court case are available in all the competing reporters.

           2)   To teach you which kinds of information can be found only in one or two of the reporters.

           3)   To familiarize you with the parts of a case.

1. Find 405 U.S. 56. What is the name of the case?
ANSWER:

2. On what date was the case decided?
ANSWER:

3. What is the docket number of the case?
ANSWER:

4. Which party is the appellant?
ANSWER:

5. Which Justices dissented in part?
ANSWER:

6. Which Justices took no part in the decision?
ANSWER:

7. Which court ruled on this case prior to the U.S. Supreme Court?
ANSWER:

8. Who argued the cause for the appellees?
ANSWER:

9. Find the Supreme Court Reporter and U.S. Supreme Court Reports—Lawyers' Edition texts of this opinion.
    a. What is the Supreme Court Reporter citation?
       ANSWER:

    b. What is the U.S. Supreme Court Reports—Lawyers' Edition citation?
       ANSWER:

To answer Questions 10-15 you will need to compare the three published versions of this opinion.

10. Examine the <u>Supreme Court Reporter</u> and <u>U.S. Supreme Court Reports-
    -Lawyers' Edition</u> versions. Which contains "Annotation References"?
    ANSWER:

11. Which of the three published versions of this opinion tell you who filed
    amicus curiae briefs? NOTE: In one service, this information is not listed
    with the opinion. State the name of the reporter and the page number on
    which you found it.
    ANSWER:

12. On which page of which published text does the first West key number and
    topic appear?
    ANSWER:

13. State the West topic and key number from the preceding question.
    ANSWER:

14. Examine the three published texts and state which provide headnotes
    (numbered, one-sentence summaries of points of law).
    ANSWER:

15. On which page of the <u>Supreme Court Reporter</u> <u>opinion</u> is there a reference
    to the nineteenth West headnote? State the volume, abbreviated reporter
    name, and page where the reference appears.
    ANSWER:

16. Using star paging, state on which page of <u>United States Reports</u> the paragraph
    from the preceding question would begin.
    ANSWER:

ASSIGNMENT II
U.S. SUPREME COURT REPORTERS AND PARTS OF A CASE
EXERCISE C

GOALS: 1) To teach you which kinds of information about a Supreme Court case are available in all the competing reporters.
2) To teach you which kinds of information can be found only in one or two of the reporters.
3) To familiarize you with the parts of a case.

1. Find 411 U.S. 1. What is the name of the case?
    ANSWER:

2. On what date was the case decided?
    ANSWER:

3. What is the docket number of the case?
    ANSWER:

4. Which party is the appellant?
    ANSWER:

5. Which Justice concurred?
    ANSWER:

6. Which Justices wrote dissenting opinions?
    ANSWER:

7. What is the citation from the lower court?
    ANSWER:

8. Who argued the cause for the appellant?
    ANSWER:

9. Find the Supreme Court Reporter and U.S. Supreme Court Reports—Lawyers' Edition texts of this opinion.
    a. What is the Supreme Court Reporter citation?
        ANSWER:

    b. What is the U.S. Supreme Court Reports—Lawyers' Edition citation?
        ANSWER:

To answer Questions 10-15 you will need to compare the three published versions of this opinion.

10. Examine the Supreme Court Reporter and U.S. Supreme Court Reports--Lawyers' Edition versions. Which contains "Annotation References"?
   ANSWER:

11. Which of the three published versions of this opinion tell you who filed amicus curiae briefs? NOTE: In one service, this information is not listed with the opinion. State the name of the reporter and the page number on which you found it.
   ANSWER:

12. On which page of which published text does the first West key number and topic appear?
   ANSWER:

13. State the West topic and key number from the preceding question.
   ANSWER:

14. Examine the three published texts and state which provide headnotes (numbered, one-sentence summaries of points of law).
   ANSWER:

15. On which page of the Supreme Court Reporter opinion is there a reference to the first West headnote? State the volume, abbreviated reporter name, and page where the reference appears.
   ANSWER:

16. Using star paging, state on which page of United States Reports the paragraph from the preceding question would begin.
   ANSWER:

GOALS: 1) To teach you which kinds of information about a Supreme Court case are available in all the competing reporters.
    2) To teach you which kinds of information can be found only in one or two of the reporters.
    3) To familiarize you with the parts of a case.

1. Find 414 U.S. 218. What is the name of the case?
ANSWER:

2. On what date was the case decided?
ANSWER:

3. What is the docket number of the case?
ANSWER:

4. Which party is the petitioner?
ANSWER:

5. Which Justice wrote the dissenting opinion?
ANSWER:

6. How many Justices dissented?
ANSWER:

7. What are the citations from the lower court?
ANSWER:

8. Who argued the cause for the respondent?
ANSWER:

9. Find the Supreme Court Reporter and U.S. Supreme Court Reports—Lawyers' Edition texts of this opinion.
    a. What is the Supreme Court Reporter citation?
      ANSWER:

    b. What is the U.S. Supreme Court Reports—Lawyers' Edition citation?
      ANSWER:

To answer Questions 10-15 you will need to compare the three published versions of this opinion.

10. Examine the <u>Supreme Court Reporter</u> and <u>U.S. Supreme Court Reports--Lawyers' Edition</u> versions. Which contains "Annotation References"?
    ANSWER:

11. Which of the three published versions of this opinion tell you who filed amicus curiae briefs? NOTE: In one service, this information is not listed with the opinion. State the name of the reporter and the page number on which you found it.
    ANSWER:

12. On which page of which published text does the first West key number and topic appear?
    ANSWER:

13. State the West topic and key number from the preceding question.
    ANSWER:

14. Examine the three published texts and state which provide headnotes (numbered, one-sentence summaries of points of law).
    ANSWER:

15. On which page of the <u>Supreme Court Reporter</u> opinion is there a reference to the first West headnote? State the volume, abbreviated reporter name, and page where the reference appears.
    ANSWER:

16. Using star paging, state on which page of <u>United States Reports</u> the paragraph from the preceding question would begin.
    ANSWER:

INTRODUCTION
TO CHAPTER III
UNITED STATES LAW WEEK, SUPREME COURT SECTION

This assignment will introduce you to United States Law Week, yet another source of U.S. Supreme Court opinions. U.S. Law Week is issued in two parts, the General Law Section and the Supreme Court Section. For this assignment you will use only the Supreme Court Section. Be sure that "Supreme Court" and not "General Law" is printed on the spines of the volumes you use.

The key to using U.S. Law Week is the docket number assigned by the Supreme Court. The Index section in the back of the U.S. Law Week volume contains a subject index, table of cases, and docket number table, but only the last refers you to the pages of U.S. Law Week on which your case appears. An essential step in using U.S. Law Week, therefore, is the conversion, via the Table of Cases index, of case names to docket numbers.

Each volume covers one term of the Supreme Court. A term runs from October through June. The 1980 Term ran from October 1980 through June 1981. The assignment requires you to use volumes for two terms.

You are also required to cite an opinion from U.S. Law Week in the format of A Uniform System of Citation, 13th ed. No specific instructions are given in A Uniform System; the best way to proceed is to find U.S. Law Week in the index of A Uniform System and look at the pages to which you are referred.

U.S. Law Week is a type of publication known as a looseleaf. Legal researchers use looseleaf services when they need extremely current information. Commerce Clearing House publishes a similar looseleaf service, the Supreme Court Bulletin, which also contains the full texts of Supreme Court opinions. These two services will usually contain an opinion within days of its publication, and you should consult them first if the opinion you need is very recent.

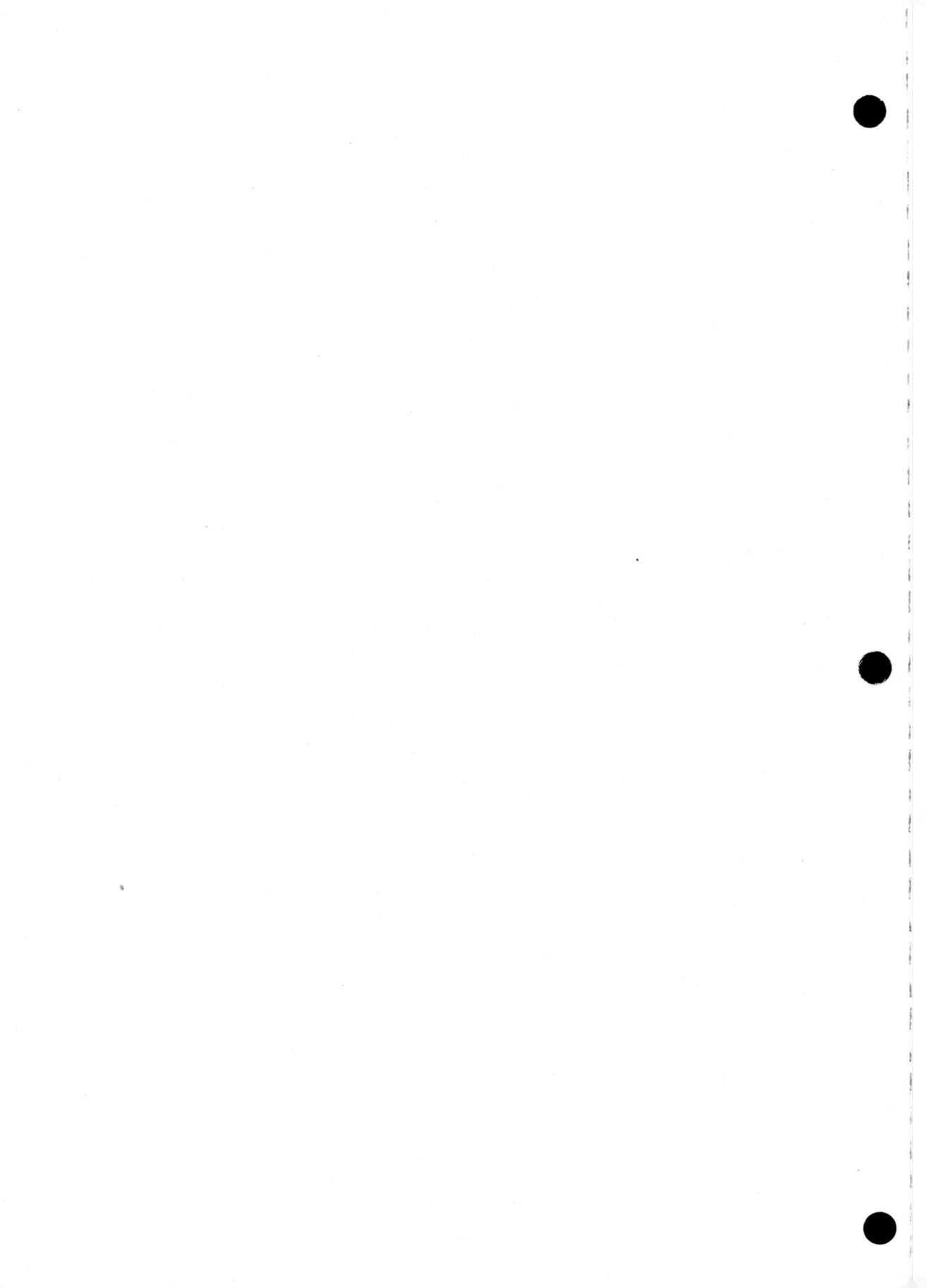

ASSIGNMENT III
UNITED STATES LAW WEEK, SUPREME COURT SECTION
EXERCISE A

GOALS: 1) To give you practice at finding cases by subject in <u>United States Law Week</u>, Supreme Court Section.

      2) To familiarize you with the information you can find regarding the progress of a case through the Supreme Court in U.S. Law Week.

      3) To give you practice at searching for information about the same case through more than one term of the Supreme Court in <u>U.S. Law Week</u>.

1.   Using the 1976-77 <u>U.S. Law Week</u>, Supreme Court Section, look for a case involving the liability of a Nevada tavern keeper when one of his customers, after being served numerous intoxicating beverages, injured a California resident on a California highway.

    a.   What is the docket number of the case?
        ANSWER:

    b.   On what page is there a summary of the case?
        ANSWER:

    c.   During the 1976 Term (remember, this covers 1976-77) did the Court grant certiorari?
        ANSWER:

    d.   Did it hear the arguments of counsel?
        ANSWER:

    e.   Did it issue an opinion?
        ANSWER:

2. Look for a case involving the 1st Amendment right of a New Hampshire Jehovah's Witness couple to cover up the motto "Live Free or Die" on their license plates.

    a. What is the docket number of the case?
       ANSWER:

    b. On what date was the case argued before the Court?
       ANSWER:

    c. Using A Uniform System of Citation, 13th ed. cite the Court's opinion as published in U.S. Law Week.
       ANSWER:

3.   a. Give the docket number for United States v. New York Telephone Co..
       ANSWER:

    b. During the 1976 Term, did the Court grant certiorari?
       ANSWER:

    c. During the 1977 Term (use the next volume of U.S. Law Week), state the date the Court heard argument.
       ANSWER:

    d. On what date was the case decided?
       ANSWER:

ASSIGNMENT III
UNITED STATES LAW WEEK, SUPREME COURT SECTION
EXERCISE B

GOALS: 1) To give you practice at finding cases by subject in <u>United States Law Week</u>, Supreme Court Section.

2) To familiarize you with the information you can find regarding the progress of a case through the Supreme Court in <u>U.S. Law Week</u>.

3) To give you practice at searching for information about the same case through more than one term of the Supreme Court in <u>U.S. Law Week</u>.

1. Using the 1977-78 <u>U.S. Law Week</u>, Supreme Court Section, look for a case involving a libel suit against a television documentary producer where the lower court found that during pre-trial discovery procedures the producer was not required to disclose his opinions and conclusions formed during his research for the documentary.

    a. What is the docket number of the case?
       ANSWER:

    b. On what page is there a summary of the case?
       ANSWER:

    c. During the 1977 Term (remember, this covers 1977-78) did the Court grant certiorari?
       ANSWER:

    d. Did it hear the arguments of counsel?
       ANSWER:

    e. Did it issue an opinion?
       ANSWER:

2. Look for a case involving the completion of a dam where respondents asked that construction of the multimillion-dollar dam be halted because it would jeopardize the continued existence of an endangered species, the snail darter.

    a. What is the docket number of the case?
    ANSWER:

    b. On what date was the case argued before the Court?
    ANSWER:

    c. Using A Uniform System of Citation, 13th ed., cite the Court's opinion as published in U.S. Law Week.
    ANSWER:

3.   a. State the docket number for Givhan v. Western Line Consolidated School District.
    ANSWER:

    b. During the 1977 Term, what action had the Court taken with respect to this case?
    ANSWER:

    c. During the 1978 Term (use the next volume of U.S. Law Week), state the date the Court heard argument.
    ANSWER:

    d. On what date was the case decided?
    ANSWER:

ASSIGNMENT III
UNITED STATES LAW WEEK, SUPREME COURT SECTION
EXERCISE C

GOALS: 1) To give you practice at finding cases by subject in United States Law Week, Supreme Court Section.
2) To familiarize you with the information you can find regarding the progress of a case through the Supreme Court in U.S. Law Week.
3) To give you practice at searching for information about the same case through more than one term of the Supreme Court in U.S. Law Week.

1. Using the 1978-79 U.S. Law Week, Supreme Court Section, look for a case deciding whether the Freedom of Information Act covers notes of telephone conversations made by a Secretary of State which he later donated to the Library of Congress.

   a. What is the docket number of the case?
   ANSWER:

   b. On what page is there a summary of the case?
   ANSWER:

   c. During the 1978 Term (remember, this covers 1978-79) did the Court grant certiorari?
   ANSWER:

   d. Did it hear the arguments of counsel?
   ANSWER:

   e. Did it issue an opinion?
   ANSWER:

2. Look for an interstate commerce case involving the transportation or shipment out of state of minnows seined within state waters.

    a. What is the docket number of the case?
    ANSWER:

    b. On what date was the case argued before the Court?
    ANSWER:

    c. Using the Uniform System of Citation, 13th ed., cite the Court's opinion as published in U.S. Law Week.
    ANSWER:

3. a. State the docket number for Whalen v. United States.
    ANSWER:

    b. During the 1978 Term, did the Court grant certiorari?
    ANSWER:

    c. During the 1979 Term (use the next volume of U.S. Law Week), state the dates the Court heard argument.
    ANSWER:

    d. On what date was the case decided?
    ANSWER:

GOALS: 1)   To give you practice at finding cases by subject in <u>United States Law Week</u>, Supreme Court Section.

         2)   To familiarize you with the information you can find regarding the progress of a case through the Supreme Court in <u>U.S. Law Week</u>.

         3)   To give you practice at searching for information about the same case through more than one term of the Supreme Court in <u>U.S. Law Week</u>.

1.   Using the 1979–80 <u>U.S. Law Week</u>, Supreme Court Section, look for a case involving an attorney for a corporate defendant who withdrew before trial and left the officers and shareholders unrepresented.

    a.   What is the docket number of the case?
        ANSWER:

    b.   On what page is there a summary of the case?
        ANSWER:

    c.   During the 1979 Term (remember, this covers 1979–1980) did the Court grant certiorari?
        ANSWER:

    d.   Did it hear the arguments of counsel?
        ANSWER:

    e.   Did it issue an opinion?
        ANSWER:

2. Look for a case holding that the IRS had the right to compel evidence in the form of handwriting exemplars.

    a. What is the docket number of the case?
    ANSWER:

    b. On what date was the case argued before the Court?
    ANSWER:

    c. Using the Uniform System of Citation, 13th ed., cite the Court's opinion as published in U.S. Law Week.
    ANSWER:

3.   a. State the docket number for Fedorenko v. United States.
    ANSWER:

    b. During the 1979 Term did the Court grant certiorari?
    ANSWER:

    c. During the 1980 Term (use the next volume of U.S. Law Week), state the date the Court heard argument.
    ANSWER:

    d. On what date was the case decided?
    ANSWER:

INTRODUCTION
TO CHAPTER IV
LOWER FEDERAL COURT REPORTS

This exercise will introduce you to the reporters for the lower federal courts--the Circuit Courts of Appeal, the District Courts, and various special courts. You will use the Federal Reporter, Federal Supplement, Federal Rules Decisions, and Federal Cases. You will be introduced to the various features of West reporters which are potential sources of information you will need either in law school or in practice. While the questions in this exercise are not themselves associated with fact patterns requiring legal solutions, any one of them could be. Notice that each question in this exercise and each table in the reporter volume would be helpful in your research activity depending on what particular piece of information or what need for a particular piece of information you begin with, i.e., that a case was decided by a court in a particular circuit, that you need to locate a case whose name you know, or that you wish to find all cases which have discussed a particular legal phrase.

Before you begin, read the section on "Lower Federal Courts" in Chapter 3 of Cohen and Berring, How to Find the Law, 8th ed. You may also find West's Law Finder pamphlet helpful.

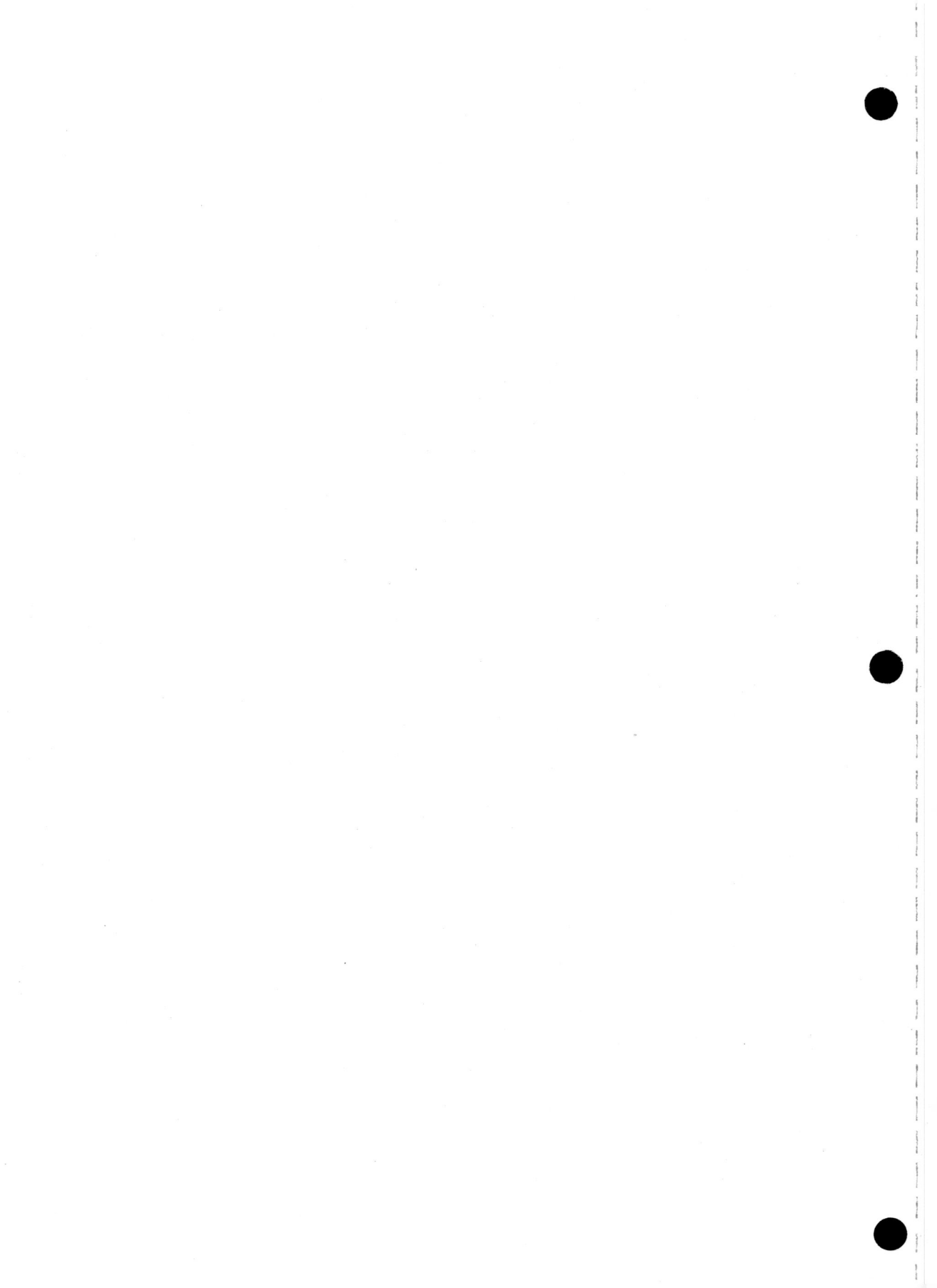

ASSIGNMENT IV
LOWER FEDERAL COURT REPORTS
EXERCISE B

GOALS: 1) To familiarize you with which court opinions are reported in the various lower federal court reporters.
2) To acquaint you with the various tables in reporter volumes which identify, for example, any cases interpreting statutes, words and phrases, or rules of procedure.
3) To introduce you to the major nineteenth century federal reporter, Federal Cases.
4) To give you practice at citing lower federal court cases in correct form.

1. Which West reporter currently reports opinions of the U.S. Court of International Trade?
ANSWER:

2. Look up 659 F.2d 163. State the full citation for the opinion according to A Uniform System of Citation, 13th ed., brief and memorandum format.
ANSWER:

3. You are seeking a case in 659 F.2d in which the defendant's name is Turner. Using the appropriate table, tell on which page the case begins.
ANSWER:

4. Using the appropriate table in 490 F. Supp., state the volume, reporter, and page number of the opinion which construes 21 U.S.C. § 1175(g).
ANSWER:

5. How many District Court decisions from the Tenth Circuit are reported in 490 F. Supp.?
ANSWER:

6. Using the appropriate section of the reporter, state the full citation of the decision in 490 F. Supp. that defines "discretionary act," according to A Uniform System of Citation, 13th ed.
ANSWER:

7. Using the appropriate table in volume 55 of Federal Rules Decisions, state the volume, reporter, and page number of a decision construing Fed. R. App. P. 39(e).
   ANSWER:

8. State the name of the opinion in 55 F.R.D. that is digested under topic and key number Federal Civil Procedure 1484.
   ANSWER:

9. Who is the author of the article on delays in criminal cases contained in 55 F.R.D.?
   ANSWER:

10. Using Federal Cases, state the full citation of Kimball v. Taylor, according to A Uniform System of Citation, 13th ed.
    ANSWER:

11. State the name of case no. 7,914.
    ANSWER:

12. Use the Digest volume of Federal Cases. What is the Federal Cases number of the opinion that appeared at 2 Southern Law Review 725?
    ANSWER:

ASSIGNMENT IV
LOWER FEDERAL COURT REPORTS
EXERCISE C

GOALS:
1) To familiarize you with which court opinions are reported in the various lower federal court reporters.
2) To acquaint you with the various tables in reporter volumes which identify, for example, any cases interpreting statutes, words and phrases, or rules of procedure.
3) To introduce you to the major nineteenth century federal reporter, Federal Cases.
4) To give you practice at citing lower federal court cases in correct form.

1. Which West reporter currently reports opinions of the Temporary Emergency Court of Appeals?
ANSWER:

2. Look up 655 F.2d 453. State the full citation for the opinion according to A Uniform System of Citation, 13th ed., brief and memorandum format.
ANSWER:

3. You are seeking a case in 655 F.2d in which the defendant's name is White. Using the appropriate table, tell on which page the case begins.
ANSWER:

4. Using the appropriate table in 495 F. Supp., state the volume, reporter, and page number of the opinion which construes 14 U.S.C. § 89(a).
ANSWER:

5. How many decisions from the Customs Court are reported in 495 F. Supp.?
ANSWER:

6. Using the appropriate section of the reporter, state the full citation of the decision in the same volume that defines "public forums," according to A Uniform System of Citation, 13th ed.
ANSWER:

7. Using the appropriate table in volume 60 of <u>Federal Rules Decisions</u>, state the volume, reporter, and page number of a decision construing Fed. R. Civ. P. 20(a).
   ANSWER:

8. State the name of the opinion in 60 F.R.D. that is digested under topic and key number Courts 107.
   ANSWER:

9. Who is the author of the article on waivers in pleas of guilty contained in 60 F.R.D.?
   ANSWER:

10. Using <u>Federal Cases</u>, state the full citation of <u>Manning v. Hoover,</u> according to <u>A Uniform System of Citation</u>, 13th ed.
    ANSWER:

11. State the name of case no. 8,951.
    ANSWER:

12. Use the Digest volume of <u>Federal Cases.</u> What is the <u>Federal Cases</u> number of the opinion that appeared at 2 Bench & Bar 65?
    ANSWER:

ASSIGNMENT IV
LOWER FEDERAL COURT REPORTS
EXERCISE D

GOALS: 1) To familiarize you with which court opinions are reported in the various lower federal court reporters.
2) To acquaint you with the various tables in reporter volumes which identify, for example, any cases interpreting statutes, words and phrases, or rules of procedure.
3) To introduce you to the major nineteenth century federal reporter, Federal Cases.
4) To give you practice at citing lower federal court cases in correct form.

1. Which West reporter that is still published today reported U.S. District Court cases prior to 1932?
ANSWER:

2. Look up 665 F.2d 500. State the full citation for the opinion according to A Uniform System of Citation, 13th ed., brief and memorandum format.
ANSWER:

3. You are seeking a case in 665 F.2d in which the defendant's name is Kendall. Using the appropriate table, tell on which page the case begins.
ANSWER:

4. Using the appropriate table in 530 F. Supp., state the volume, reporter, and page number of the opinion which construes 11 U.S.C. § 32(f)(2).
ANSWER:

5. How many District Court decisions from the Fourth Circuit are reported in 530 F. Supp.?
ANSWER:

6. Using the appropriate section of the reporter, state the full citation of the decision in 530 F. Supp. that defines "taking," according to A Uniform System of Citation, 13th ed.
ANSWER:

7. Using the appropriate table in volume 65 of <u>Federal Rules Decisions</u>, state the volume, reporter, and page number of a decision construing Fed. R. Crim. P. 16(c).
   ANSWER:

8. State the name of the opinion in 65 F.R.D. that is digested under topic and key number Federal Civil Procedure 103.
   ANSWER:

9. Who is the author of the article on the new Federal Rules of Evidence contained in 65 F.R.D.?
   ANSWER:

10. Using <u>Federal Cases</u>, state the full citation of <u>In re O'Bannon</u>, according to <u>A Uniform System of Citation</u>, 13th ed.
    ANSWER:

11. State the name of case no. 10,308.
    ANSWER:

12. Use the Digest volume of <u>Federal Cases</u>. What is the <u>Federal Cases</u> number of the opinion that appeared at 1 Pacific Law Magazine 267?
    ANSWER:

INTRODUCTION
TO CHAPTER V
STATE AND REGIONAL COURT REPORTS

The purpose of this assignment is to familiarize you with state and regional court reporters. You will examine an official state reports volume and a volume of a West regional reporter. You will discover one way to obtain an unofficial parallel citation for an official citation. You should gain a rough idea of which states' decisions can be found in which regional reporters, and learn how to cite state nominative reports.

To complete this exercise you will need to use A Uniform System of Citation, 13th ed., the National Reporter Blue Book, a specified state offical reports volume, and a specified regional reporter volume. You may also choose to use either Cohen and Berring, How to Find the Law, 8th ed., or West's Law Finder.

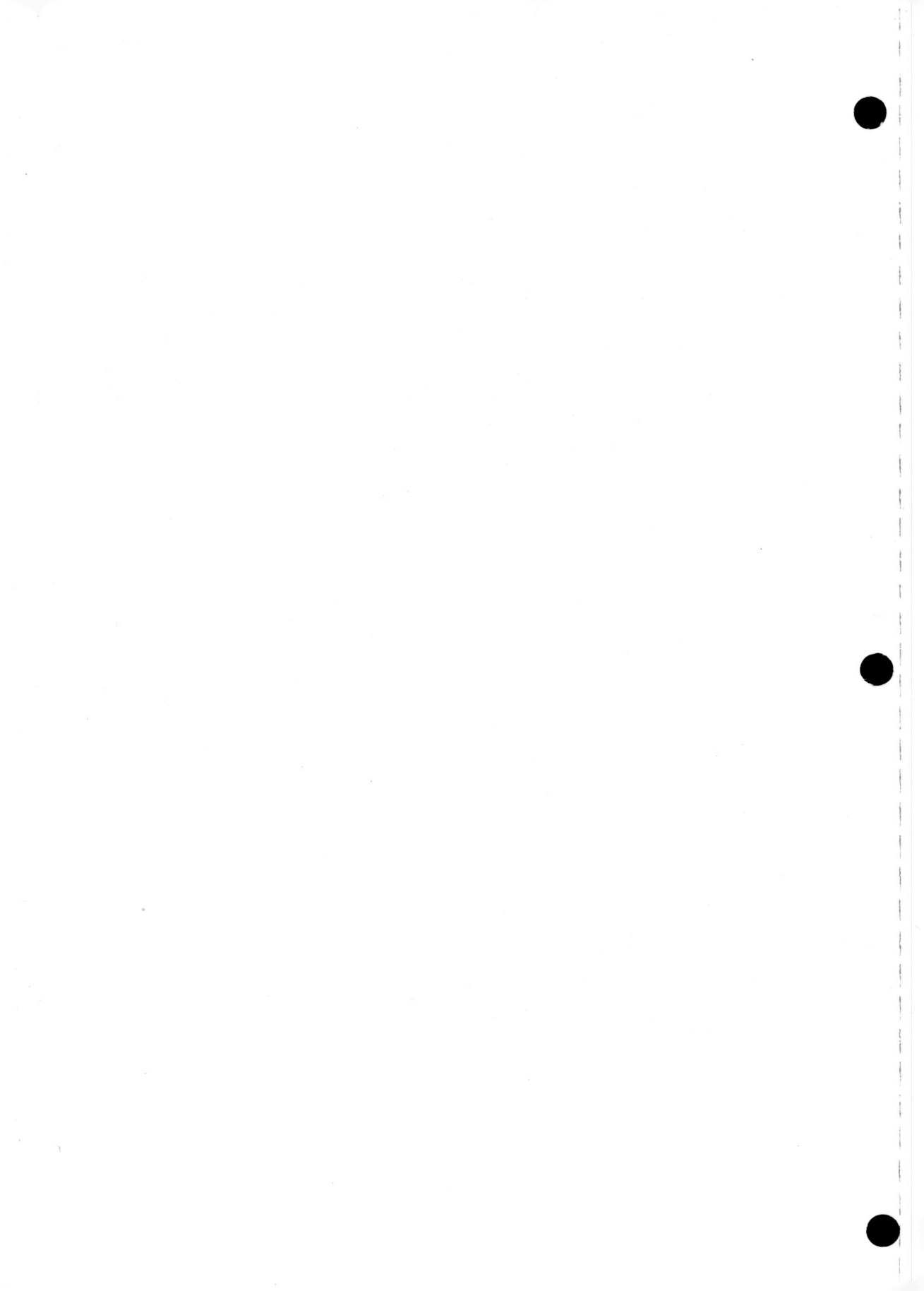

ASSIGNMENT V
STATE AND REGIONAL COURT REPORTS
EXERCISE A

GOALS: 1) To make you aware of the differences and similarities between official and unofficial state reports.
          2) To teach you one method of finding an unofficial parallel citation to an official citation.
          3) To acquaint you with the format and features of regional reporters.
          4) To give you practice in citing state nominative reports.

1. Using either Cohen and Berring, How to Find the Law, 8th ed., A Uniform System of Citation, 13th ed., or West's Law Finder, state the regional reporters in which the following states' reports are found:

   a. Alabama   **ANSWER:**

   b. Connecticut   **ANSWER:**

   c. Illinois   **ANSWER:**

   d. Maine   **ANSWER:**

   e. Missouri   **ANSWER:**

2. Using the National Reporter Blue Book, state the unofficial parallel citations to the official citations listed below. Abbreviate the names of the unofficial reporters according to A Uniform System of Citation, 13th ed.

   a. 20 Colo. App. 61   **ANSWER:**

   b. 50 Nev. 80   **ANSWER:**

   c. 138 Neb. 552   **ANSWER:**

   d. 240 N.C. 472   **ANSWER:**

   e. 64 Ill. App. 3d 273   **ANSWER:**

3. Can you use the National Reporter Blue Book to find the official parallel citation if you already have the unofficial citation?
   ANSWER:

4. Examine vol. 9 of the California Reports, 3d Series, if your library has
    that volume, and use it to answer the following questions:

    a. Who is the Reporter of Decisions?
        ANSWER:

    b. What is the name of the court of last resort in California?
        ANSWER:

    c. On what page could you discover which local ordinances were cited in
        this volume?
        ANSWER:

    d. Does this volume contain headnotes?
        ANSWER:

    f. If so, do the headnotes also appear in a separately published digest?
        ANSWER:

    f. Using only this volume, can you find in it parallel citations to the
        regional reporter?
        ANSWER:

5. Examine vol. 399 of the Atlantic Reporter, 2d Series, and use it to answer
    the following questions:

    a. Which states are covered by the Atlantic Reporter?
        ANSWER:

    b. What is the official parallel citation to Karcher v. Byrne, 399 A.2d 644?
        ANSWER:

      c.   Does 399 A.2d contain references to the official parallel citation for every case reported in it?
ANSWER:

      d.   Cite the decision in this volume that is indexed under the topic and key number Criminal Law 372(7).
ANSWER:

6.   Using A Uniform System of Citation, 13th ed., state the volumes of the nominative reporters to which the official reporter volumes correspond (e.g. the answer to 15 Va. would be 1 Munf.):

      a.   24 Del.   **ANSWER:**

      b.   8 D.C.   **ANSWER:**

      c.   64 Ky.   **ANSWER:**

      d.   83 Mass.   **ANSWER:**

      e.   9 Miss.   **ANSWER:**

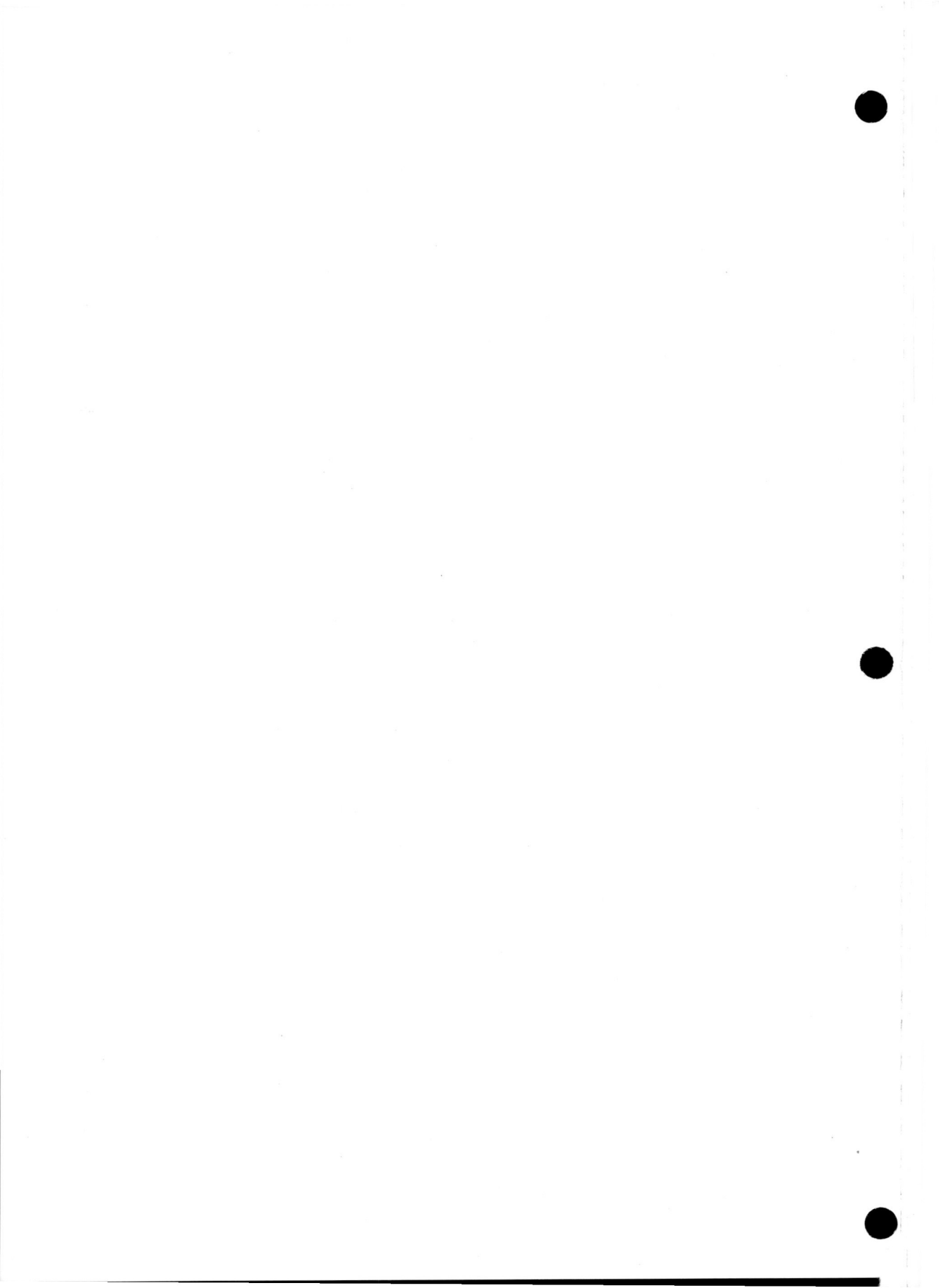

GOALS: 1) To make you aware of the differences and similarities between official and unofficial state reports.
2) To teach you one method of finding an unofficial parallel citation to an official citation.
3) To acquaint you with the format and features of regional reporters.
4) To give you practice in citing state nominative reports.

1. Using either Cohen and Berring, How to Find the Law, 8th ed., A Uniform System of Citation, 13th ed., or West's Law Finder, state the regional reporters in which the following states' reports are found:

   a. Arizona   **ANSWER:**

   b. Florida   **ANSWER:**

   c. Iowa   **ANSWER:**

   d. New Hampshire   **ANSWER:**

   e. North Carolina   **ANSWER:**

2. Using the National Reporter Blue Book, state the unofficial parallel citations to the official citations listed below. Abbreviate the names of the unofficial reporters according to A Uniform System of Citation, 13th ed.

   a. 129 Ill. 298   **ANSWER:**

   b. 16 La. App. 177   **ANSWER:**

   c. 15 N.J. Super. 274   **ANSWER:**

   d. 64 Cal. 2d 591   **ANSWER:**

   e. 254 Ind. 100   **ANSWER:**

3. Can you use the National Reporter Blue Book to find the official parallel citation if you already have the unofficial citation?
   ANSWER:

4. Examine vol. 89 of the Illinois Reports 2d Series, if your library has that volume, and use it to answer the following questions:

    a. Who is the Reporter of Decisions?
    ANSWER:

    b. What is the name of the court of last resort in Illinois?
    ANSWER:

    c. How many cases in this volume concern contempt?
    ANSWER:

    d. Does this volume contain headnotes?
    ANSWER:

    e. If so, do the headnotes also appear in a separately published digest?
    ANSWER:

    f. Using only this volume, can you find in it parallel citations to the regional reporter?
    ANSWER:

5. Examine vol. 318 of the North Western Reporter, 2d Series, and use it to answer the following questions:

    a. Which states are covered by the North Western Reporter?
    ANSWER:

    b. What is the official citation to Hengen v. Hengen, 318 N.W.2d 269?
    ANSWER:

      c.   Does 318 N.W.2d contain references to the official parallel citation to every case reported in it?
ANSWER:

      d.   Cite the decision in this volume that is indexed under the topic and key number Divorce 241.
ANSWER:

6.   Using <u>A Uniform System of Citation,</u> 13th ed., state the volumes of the nominative reporters to which the official reporter volumes correspond (e.g. the answer to 15 Va. would be 1 Munf.):

      a.   15 Del.   **ANSWER:**

      b.   6 Ill.   **ANSWER:**

      c.   58 Ky.   **ANSWER:**

      d.   42 Mass.   **ANSWER:**

      e.   1 Miss.   **ANSWER:**

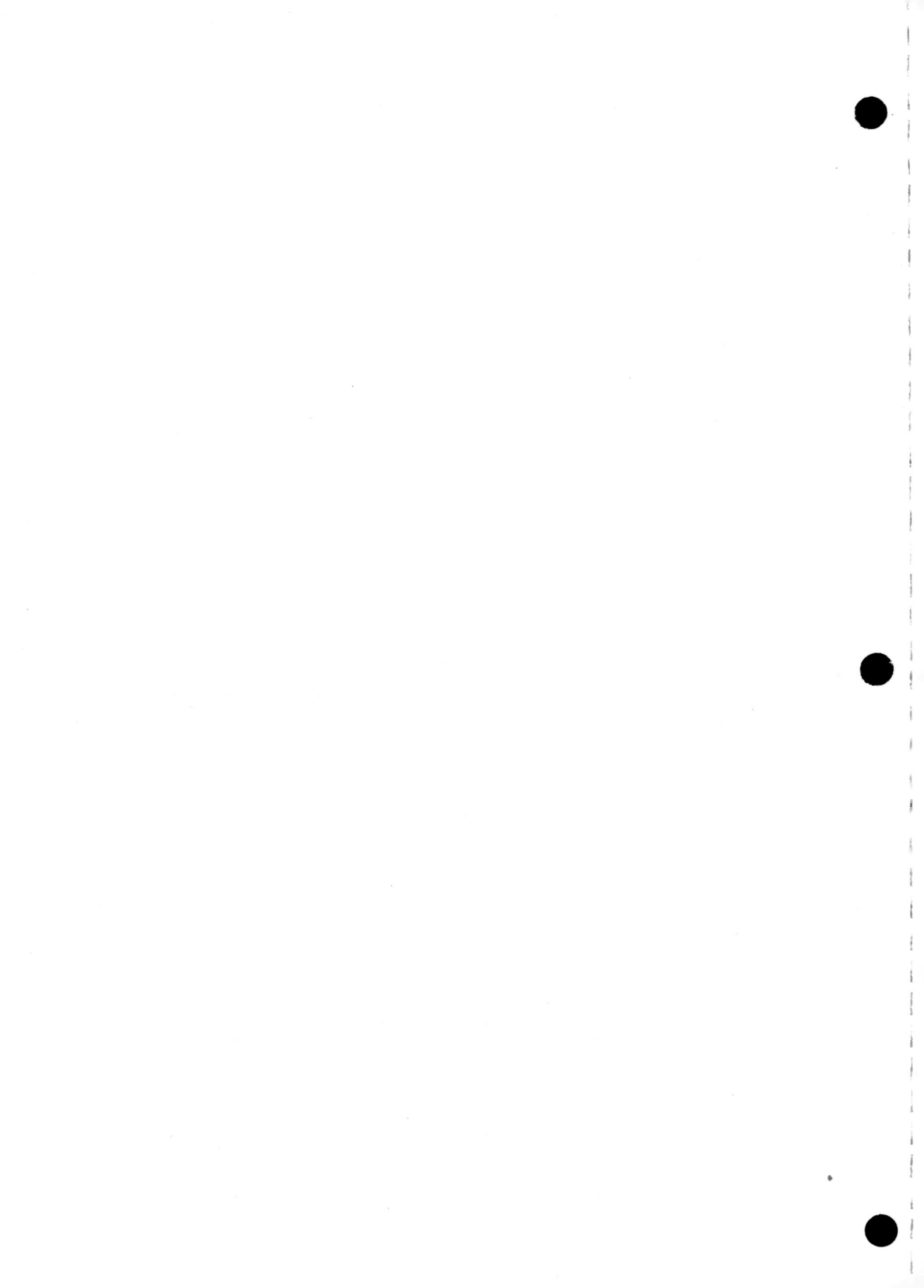

ASSIGNMENT V
STATE AND REGIONAL COURT REPORTS
EXERCISE D

GOALS: 1) To make you aware of the differences and similarities between official and unofficial state reports.
2) To teach you one method of finding an unofficial parallel citation to an official citation.
3) To acquaint you with the format and features of regional reporters.
4) To give you practice in citing state nominative reports.

1. Using either Cohen and Berring, How to Find the Law, 8th ed., A Uniform System of Citation, 13th ed., or West's Law Finder, state the regional reporters in which the following states' reports are found:

    a. Arkansas   **ANSWER:**

    b. Georgia   **ANSWER:**

    c. Kansas   **ANSWER:**

    d. New Jersey   **ANSWER:**

    e. New York   **ANSWER:**

2. Using the National Reporter Blue Book, state the unofficial parallel citations to the official citations listed below. Abbreviate the names of the unofficial reporters according to A Uniform System of Citation, 13th ed.

    a. 73 Iowa 236   **ANSWER:**

    b. 229 Mo. App. 686   **ANSWER:**

    c. 53 Cal. 2d 558   **ANSWER:**

    d. 12 Ohio App. 2d 178   **ANSWER:**

    e. 2 Mass. App. Ct. 5   **ANSWER:**

3. Can you use the National Reporter Blue Book to find the official parallel citation if you already have the unofficial citation?
ANSWER:

4. Examine vol. 289 of the Maryland Reports, if your library has that volume, and use it to answer the following questions:

    a. Who is the State Reporter?
        ANSWER:

    b. What is the name of the court of last resort in Maryland?
        ANSWER:

    c. On which pages could you discover which local ordinances were cited in this volume?
        ANSWER:

    d. Does this volume contain headnotes?
        ANSWER:

    e. If so, do the headnotes also appear in a separately published digest?
        ANSWER:

    f. Using only this volume, can you find in it parallel citations to the regional reporter?
        ANSWER:

5. Examine vol. 646 of the Pacific Reporter, 2d Series, and use it to answer the following questions:

    a. Which states are covered by the Pacific Reporter?
        ANSWER:

    b. What is the official parallel citation to State v. Burdick, 646 P.2d 91?
        ANSWER:

    c.   Does 646 P.2d contain references to the official parallel citation for every case reported in it?
ANSWER:

    d.   Cite the decision in this volume that is indexed under the topic and key number Criminal Law 260.7.
ANSWER:

6.   Using <u>A Uniform System of Citation</u>, 13th ed., state the volumes of the nominative reporters to which the official reporter volumes correspond (e.g. the answer to 15 Va. would be 1 Munf.):

    a.   6 Del.   **ANSWER:**

    b.   2 Ill.   **ANSWER:**

    c.   40 Ky.   **ANSWER:**

    d.   18 Mass.   **ANSWER:**

    e.   28 Va.   **ANSWER:**

INTRODUCTION
TO CHAPTER VI
AMERICAN DIGEST SYSTEM

The American Digest System includes headnotes from all federal and state cases reported by West in the National Reporter System. It is a massive and sometimes daunting set, composed of the Century Digest, the Decennial Digests (published every ten years from 1906 until 1981 when the first five-year Decennial was issued), and the General Digest, which indexes cases decided since the last Decennial.

You will begin by using the "descriptive word" approach to find a case. You will ascertain under which topics the case was digested. One of those topics is no longer used by West. You will learn how to tell this, and how to find out what the new topic is.

You will use the General Digests, which update the Decennials and are themselves superseded by new Decennials which cumulate earlier General Digests. Finally, you will learn how to convert back and forth from the West topics and key numbers to the Century Digest topic and number system.

Before beginning this assignment, read about the American Digest System in Chapter 5 of Cohen and Berring, How to Find the Law, 8th ed. Read about digests in West's Law Finder. You may wish to keep a copy of it at hand as you complete the assignment.

ASSIGNMENT VI
AMERICAN DIGEST SYSTEM
EXERCISE B

GOALS: 1) To give you experience at finding a case using the descriptive word method.

2) To enable you to understand how to continue your research when West has changed your topic and key number.

3) To enable you to perceive how the Tables in the General Digest work.

4) To give you practice at converting back and forth between First Decennial topics and key numbers and the Century Digest numbering system.

1. Using the appropriate Decennial Digest, find a 1929 Iowa case digest concerning seisin of the wife or husband as a requisite for curtesy. What is the name of the case?
ANSWER:

2. Find the case name from Question 1 in the Table of Cases. Under what topics and key numbers is the case digested? List all of them.
ANSWER:

3. Keeping in mind the first topic from Question 2, find it in the Ninth Decennial Digest Part I. To what new topic are you referred?
ANSWER:

4. Look up this topic in the Ninth Decennial Digest. At its beginning, there is a table which refers one from prior topics and key numbers to the new or expanded topic and key numbers. What new topic and key number(s) correspond to your discontinued topic and its key number from Question 2?
ANSWER:

5. Under what topic(s) and key number(s) in vol. 5 of the General Digest, Sixth Series is Katz v. Worker's Compensation Appeals Board digested?
ANSWER:

6. Use the Table of Cases Affirmed, Etc. What was the disposition of the case from Question 5 on appeal?
    ANSWER:

7. Use the Table of Key Numbers in Volume 10 of the General Digest, Sixth Series. If you were seeking cases digested under Shipping 131, in which volumes would you find them?
    ANSWER:

8. If you had been working with the topic and key number Municipal Corporations § 1035 in the First Decennial Digest and wished to convert to the Century Digest numbering system, which topic and number(s) would you use? Begin by finding the topic and number in the First Decennial.
    ANSWER:

9. If you had searched under Grand Jury § 37 in the Century Digest and wished to continue in the First Decennial Digest, under which topic and key number(s) would you search? Use the table in Vol. 21 of the First Decennial.
    ANSWER:

ASSIGNMENT VI
AMERICAN DIGEST SYSTEM
EXERCISE C

GOALS:
1) To give you experience at finding a case using the descriptive word method.
2) To enable you to understand how to continue your research when West has changed your topic and key number.
3) To enable you to perceive how the Tables in the General Digest work.
4) To give you practice at converting back and forth between First Decennial topics and key numbers and the Century Digest numbering system.

1. Using the appropriate Decennial Digest, find a 1944 Pennsylvania District Court case digest concerning a master's liability for a servant's injuries where the injury was caused by the defective boom on a crane. What is the name of the case?
   ANSWER:

2. Find the case name from Question 1 in the Table of Cases. Under what topics and key numbers is the case digested? List all of them.
   ANSWER:

3. Keeping in mind the fourth topic from Question 2, find it in the Ninth Decennial Digest Part I. To what new topic are you referred?
   ANSWER:

4. Look up this topic in the Ninth Decennial Digest. At its beginning, there is a table which refers one from prior topics and key numbers to the new or expanded topic and key numbers. What new topic and key number(s) correspond to your discontinued topic and its first key number from Question 2?
   ANSWER:

5. Under what topic(s) and key number(s) in vol. 4 of the General Digest, Sixth Series is Anaconda Co. v. Franchise Tax Board digested?
   ANSWER:

6.   Use the Table of Cases Affirmed, Etc. in Vol. 10 of the General Digest, Sixth Series. What was the disposition of the case from Question 5 on appeal?
      ANSWER:

7.   Use the Table of Key Numbers in Volume 10 of the General Digest, Sixth Series. If you were seeking cases digested under Mental Health 443, in which volumes would you find them?
      ANSWER:

8.   If you had been working with the topic and key number Hawkers and Peddlers § 5 in the First Decennial Digest and wished to convert to the Century Digest numbering system, which topic and number(s) would you use? Begin by finding the topic and number in the First Decennial.
      ANSWER:

9.   If you had searched under Mortgages § 1078 in the Century Digest and wished to continue in the First Decennial, under which topic and key number(s) would you search? Use the table in Vol. 21 of the First Decennial.
      ANSWER:

ASSIGNMENT VI
AMERICAN DIGEST SYSTEM
EXERCISE D

GOALS: 1) To give you experience at finding a case using the descriptive word method.

2) To enable you to understand how to continue your research when West has changed your topic and key number.

3) To enable you to perceive how the Tables in the General Digest work.

4) To give you practice at converting back and forth between First Decennial topics and key numbers and the Century Digest numbering system.

1. Using the Sixth Decennial Digest, find a Michigan case digested under pawnbrokers' charges. What is the name of the case?
ANSWER:

2. Find the case name from Question 1 in the Table of Cases. Under what topics and key numbers is the case digested? List all of them.
ANSWER:

3. Keeping in mind the third topic from Question 2, find it in the Ninth Decennial Digest Part I. To what new topic are you referred?
ANSWER:

4. Look up this topic in the Ninth Decennial Digest. At its beginning, there is a table which refers one from prior topics and key numbers to the new or expanded topic and key numbers. What new topic and key number(s) correspond to your discontinued topic and its key number from Question 2?
ANSWER:

5. Under what topic(s) and key number(s) in vol. 6 of the General Digest, Sixth Series is Wilson v. Wilson (the Federal Circuit Court of Appeals case) digested?
ANSWER:

6. Use the Table of Cases Affirmed, Etc. in Volume 15 of the General Digest, Sixth Series. What action did the U.S. Supreme Court take with respect to the case from Question 5?
   ANSWER:

7. Use the Table of Key Numbers in Volume 10 of the General Digest, Sixth Series. If you were seeking cases digested under Zoning and Planning 8, in which volumes would you find them?
   ANSWER:

8. If you had been working with the topic and key number Scire Facias § 4 in the First Decennial Digest and wished to convert to the Century Digest numbering system, which topic and number(s) would you use? Begin by finding the topic and number in the First Decennial.
   ANSWER:

9. If you had searched under Good Will § 8 in the Century Digest and wished to continue in the First Decennial Digest, under which topic and key number(s) would you search? Use the table in Vol. 21 of the First Decennial.
   ANSWER:

INTRODUCTION
TO CHAPTER VII
FEDERAL DIGESTS

This assignment introduces you to the three federal digests: the Federal Digest, the Modern Federal Practice Digest, and the Federal Practice Digest 2d. They are all published by West and cover different time periods, but use the same key numbering system. You will use all of the digests.

After completing this chapter, you will have used both the American Digest System and the federal digests. All cases in the latter are also contained in the former. You should use the federal digests when you want to limit your results to Supreme Court and lower federal court cases, just as you would use the Supreme Court digests when you want to limit your search to Supreme Court cases. However, even if this is your goal, you should always update your search in the General Digests. They are published more frequently than are the paper supplements to the Federal Practice Digest 2d, and so contain more recent cases most of the time.

Before beginning this assignment, read about the federal digests in Chapter 5 of Cohen and Berring, How to Find the Law, 8th ed. You should also read the pertinent parts of West's Law Finder. We suggest that you have it at hand as you complete this assignment.

ASSIGNMENT VII
FEDERAL DIGESTS
EXERCISE B

GOALS: 1) To familiarize you with the time periods covered by the respective federal digests.
2) To give you practice at finding digested cases using the topic outline method.
3) To give you practice at tracing a topic and key number through several digests, as you will need to do when you want to identify all cases decided on a particular point of law.

1. You are searching for a 1953 federal case in which the defendant's name is Quilop. Which West federal digest should you use?
ANSWER:

2. What is the name of the case?
ANSWER:

3. Under what topic and key number is the case digested?
ANSWER:

4. Find the topic from Question 3 in the digest. Study the analysis and outline at the beginning of the topic. Do not use the Descriptive Word Index. If you wished to find case digests on misleading, confusing, or contradictory jury instructions concerning murder charges, which topic and key number would you use?
ANSWER:

5. To see whether there were any pre–1939 federal cases digested under the topic and key number from Question 3, which digest would you use?
ANSWER:

6. State the name of the U.S. Supreme Court case which you find in the digest from Question 5 digested under the topic and key number from Question 3.
    ANSWER:

7. To see whether any pertinent cases were published during the 1960s or later, which digest would you use?
    ANSWER:

8. Find the topic and key number from Question 3 in the digest from Question 7. How many district court cases digested under the topic were published during the 1970s?
    ANSWER:

9. Using the Federal Practice Digest 2d, state the names of the opinions that define "Good Samaritan."
    ANSWER:

ASSIGNMENT VII
FEDERAL DIGESTS
EXERCISE C

GOALS: 1) To familiarize you with the time periods covered by the respective federal digests.

2) To give you practice at finding digested cases using the topic outline method.

3) To give you practice at tracing a topic and key number through several digests, as you will need to do when you want to identify all cases decided on a particular point of law.

1. You are searching for a 1975 federal case in which the defendant's name is Brisco. Which West federal digest should you use?
ANSWER:

2. What is the name of the case?
ANSWER:

3. What is the <u>first</u> topic and key number under which the case is digested?
ANSWER:

4. Find the topic from Question 3 in the digest. Study the analysis and outline at the beginning of the topic. Do not use the Descriptive Word Index. If you wished to find case digests on the amendment of the Constitution of the United States, which topic and key number would you use?
ANSWER:

5. To see whether there were any pre–1939 federal cases digested under the topic and key number from Question 4, which digest would you use?
ANSWER:

6. Using the digest from Question 5 and the topic and key number from Question 4, state the name of a U.S. Supreme Court case dealing with the Nineteenth Amendment.
   ANSWER:

7. If you wished to find federal cases digested under the topic and key number from Question 4 and published during the 1940s and 1950s, which digest would you use?
   ANSWER:

8. Find the topic and key number from Question 4 in the digest from Question 7. Are any cases digested under it?
   ANSWER:

9. Using the <u>Federal Digest</u>, state the name of the opinion that defines "scab."
   ANSWER:

ASSIGNMENT VII
FEDERAL DIGESTS
EXERCISE D

GOALS: 1) To familiarize you with the time periods covered by the respective federal digests.
2) To give you practice at finding digested cases using the topic outline method.
3) To give you practice at tracing a topic and key number through several digests, as you will need to do when you want to identify all cases decided on a particular point of law.

1. You are searching for a 1924 federal case in which the defendant's name is Qvale. Which West federal digest should you use?
ANSWER:

2. What is the name of the case?
ANSWER:

3. Under what topic and key number is the case digested?
ANSWER:

4. Find the topic from Question 3 in the digest. Study the analysis and outline at the beginning of the topic. Do not use the Descriptive Word Index. If you wished to find case digests on claims against the U.S. by subjects of a foreign government, which topic and key number would you use?
ANSWER:

5. To see whether any federal cases digested under the topic and key number in Question 4 were published during the 1940s and 1950s, which digest would you use?
ANSWER:

6. Find the topic and key number from Question 4 in the digest from Question 5. Were any cases digested under it published during the 1950s?
    ANSWER:

7. To see whether any pertinent federal cases were published during the 1960s or later, which digest would you use?
    ANSWER:

8. Use the digest from Question 7 and the topic and key number from Question 4. What was the foreign country of the claimant of the 1963 case therein?
    ANSWER:

9. Using the <u>Modern Federal Practice Digest</u>, state the name of the opinion that defines "goggles."
    ANSWER:

INTRODUCTION
TO CHAPTER VIII
SUPREME COURT DIGESTS

The following assignment will acquaint you with the two U.S. Supreme Court digests, the West Supreme Court Digest and the U.S. Supreme Court Digest—Lawyers' Edition. You should use these digests when you are seeking only Supreme Court cases.

The Supreme Court digests bring together not only customary features such as word indexes, topic outlines, and tables of cases, but also provide less common approaches through words and phrases tables and popular name tables. In addition, the Lawyers' Edition digest provides the full text of federal court rules and the West digest uses the familiar key numbering system.

You might assume that the words and phrases tables and popular name tables would be indistinguishable in the two Supreme Court digests. However, you will learn through this exercise that indexing terms and the case digests listed under specific topics in the two digests are sufficiently different so that when searching for Supreme Court cases, it is advisable to search both, if they are available in your library.

Before beginning this assignment, read about the digests in West's Law Finder and The Living Law. Also read about them in Chapter 5 of Cohen and Berring, How to Find the Law, 8th ed.

GOALS: 1) To give you practice at using the descriptive word method to locate case digests.
   2) To give you practice at using special tables and unique features such as court rules in the two Supreme Court digests, since the tables and features are sometimes hard to locate.
   3) To make you aware that you may miss case digests relevant to your research inquiry if you use only one of the Supreme Court digests.
   4) To give you practice at using a digest which does not contain West key numbers.

1. Assume you are looking for the Social Security Case(s), but do not know the actual name(s). State the name(s) of the case(s) to which the U.S. Supreme Court Digests—Lawyers' Edition refers you. Popular names are found in the Table of Cases.
   ANSWER:

2. Does the West Supreme Court Digest refer you to any additional Social Security Cases? If so, state their names. A Popular Name Table is found at the end of Vol. 15.
   ANSWER:

3. In which of the two digests would you find the text of the Federal Rules of Evidence?
   ANSWER:

4. Find a 1942 case digest which holds that a state statute providing for the sterilization of habitual criminals is unconstitutional. Use the word indexes in both digests. What is the name of the case?
   ANSWER:

5. Under what indexing term or descriptive word in the West Supreme Court Digest Descriptive Word Index did you find a reference to the topic and key number?
   ANSWER:

6. Under what topic and key number in the West <u>Supreme Court Digest</u> did you find the case?
   ANSWER:

7. Under what indexing term or descriptive word in the <u>U.S. Supreme Court Digest—Lawyers' Edition</u> Word Index did you find a reference to the topic?
   ANSWER:

8. Under what topic and number did you find the case in the <u>U.S. Supreme Court Digest—Lawyers' Edition?</u>
   ANSWER:

9. State the name of the opinion that defines "pure speech." Remember that to find cases which define terms you must use a words and phrases table. In the West digest this table is located in Vol. 15. In the Lawyers' Edition digest the words and phrases table is found in Vol. 14 of the actual digest, under "words and phrases."
   ANSWER:

10. In which digest did you locate the answer to Question 9?
    ANSWER:

ASSIGNMENT VIII
SUPREME COURT DIGESTS
EXERCISE C

GOALS:
1) To give you practice at using the descriptive word method to locate case digests.
2) To give you practice at using special tables and unique features such as court rules in the two Supreme Court digests, since the tables and features are sometimes hard to locate.
3) To make you aware that you may miss case digests relevant to your research inquiry if you use only one of the Supreme Court digests.
4) To give you practice at using a digest which does not contain West key numbers.

1. Assume you are looking for the Mann Act Case(s) but do not know the actual name(s). State the name(s) of the case(s) to which the U.S. Supreme Court Digest—Lawyers' Edition refers you. Popular names are found in the Table of Cases.
    ANSWER:

2. Does the West Supreme Court Digest refer you to any additional Mann Act Cases? If so, state their names. A Popular Name Table is found at the end of Vol. 15.
    ANSWER:

3. In which of the two digests would you find the text of the U.S. Court of Appeals Rules?
    ANSWER:

4. Find a 1967 case digest which holds that a state cannot infringe upon the rights of individuals of different races to marry. Use the word indexes in both digests. What is the name of the case?
    ANSWER:

5. Under what indexing term or descriptive word in the West Supreme Court Digest Descriptive Word Index did you find a reference to the topic and key number?
    ANSWER:

6. Under what topic and key number in the West <u>Supreme Court Digest</u> did you find the case?
   ANSWER:

7. Under what indexing term or descriptive word in the <u>U.S. Supreme Court Digest--Lawyers' Edition</u> Word Index did you find a reference to the topic?
   ANSWER:

8. Under what topic and number did you find the case in the <u>U.S. Supreme Court Digest—Lawyers' Edition</u>?
   ANSWER:

9. State the name of the opinion that defines "rattoons." Remember that to find cases which define terms you must use a words and phrases table. In the West digest this table is located in vol. 15. In the Lawyers' Edition digest the words and phrases table is found in vol. 14 of the actual digest, under "Words and Phrases."
   ANSWER:

10. In which digest did you locate the answer to Question 9?
    ANSWER:

ASSIGNMENT VIII
SUPREME COURT DIGESTS
EXERCISE D

GOALS: 1) To give you practice at using the descriptive word method to locate case digests.

2) To give you practice at using special tables and unique features such as court rules in the two Supreme Court digests, since the tables and features are sometimes hard to locate.

3) To make you aware that you may miss case digests relevant to your research inquiry if you use only one of the Supreme Court digests.

4) To give you practice at using a digest which does not contain West key numbers.

1. Assume you are looking for the Lottery Case(s), but do not know the actual name(s). State the name(s) of the case(s) to which the U.S. Supreme Court Digest—Lawyers' Edition refers you. Popular names are found in the Table of Cases.
ANSWER:

2. Does the West Supreme Court Digest refer you to any additional Lottery Cases? If so, state their names. A Popular Name Table is found at the end of Vol. 15.
ANSWER:

3. In which of the two digests would you find the text of the Federal Rules of Civil Procedure?
ANSWER:

4. Find a 1976 case digest which holds that a state statute requiring mandatory retirement of state police at age 50 is valid. What is the name of the case? Use the word indexes in both digests.
ANSWER:

5. Under what indexing term or descriptive word in the West Supreme Court Digest Descriptive Word Index did you find a reference to the topic and key number?
ANSWER:

6. Under what topic and key number in the West <u>Supreme Court Digest</u> did you find the case?
ANSWER:

7. Under what indexing term or descriptive word in the <u>U.S. Supreme Court Digest—Lawyers' Edition</u> Word Index did you find a reference to the topic?
ANSWER:

8. Under what topic and number did you find the case in the <u>U.S. Supreme Court Digest—Lawyers' Edition</u>?
ANSWER:

9. State the name of the opinion that defines "hard-core pornography." Remember that to find cases which define terms you must use a words and phrases table. In the West digest this table is located in vol. 15. In the Lawyers' Edition digest the words and phrases table is found in vol. 14 of the actual digest, under "words and phrases."
ANSWER:

10. In which digest did you locate the answer to Question 9?
ANSWER:

INTRODUCTION
TO CHAPTER IX
AMERICAN LAW REPORTS

The following assignment will acquaint you with the American Law Reports (A.L.R.) and American Law Reports—Federal (A.L.R. Fed.) These sets are annotated law reports. They contain the full texts of selected court cases; however they are less often used for the texts of the decisions reported than for the annotations accompanying the reported decisions. Annotations are detailed explanatory essays on the current state of the law in a given area. Preceding each annotation is printed the full text of a case. Every annotation contains cross references to other Lawyers Co-op publications and to other annotations. Often the annotation includes a Table of Jurisdictions so that one may see at a glance whether a certain jurisdiction has any law relevant to the topic and where in the annotation the law of that jurisdiction is discussed. A.L.R. Fed. covers federal law. Both A.L.R. and A.L.R. Fed. annotations tend to concern case law more than statutory law.

Before beginning the assignment read Chapter 4 of Cohen and Berring, How to Find the Law, 8th ed., and refer to The Living Law for instructions on how to update an annotation, etc.

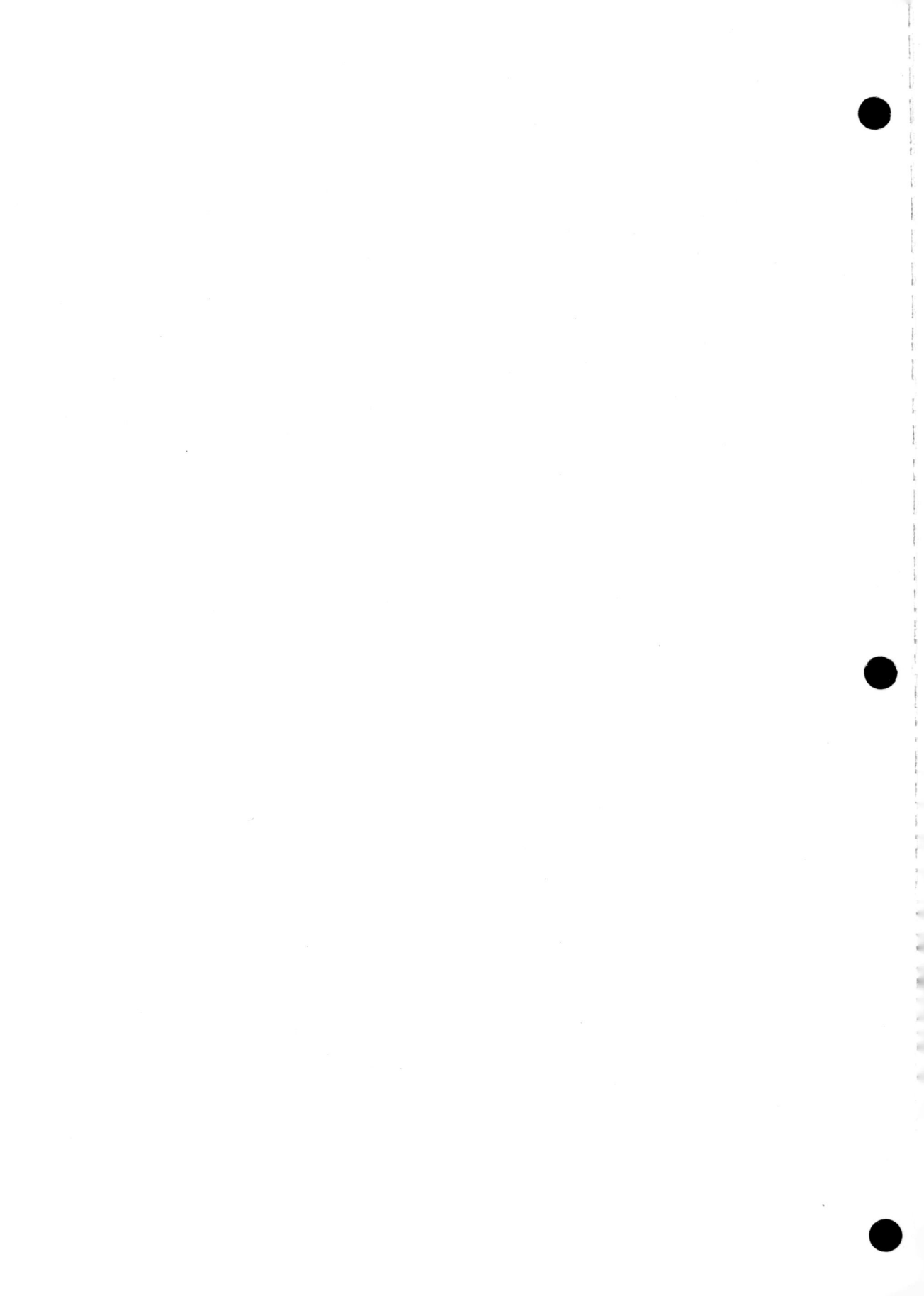

ASSIGNMENT IX
AMERICAN LAW REPORTS
EXERCISE B

GOALS: 1)   To give you practice at using the A.L.R. indexes.
2)   To make you familiar with parts of an annotation and the kinds of information regularly available in annotations.
3)   To enable you to determine the current status of an annotation.
4)   To enable you to find later cases relevant to an annotation.
5)   To show you how to determine whether particular opinions have been printed in A.L.R.

In this assignment you will be using various volumes of American Law Reports (A.L.R.) and American Law Reports—Federal (A.L.R. Fed.). "Cite" means to give all available information in the correct format, but not to seek any information not given you by the A.L.R. citation.

1.   Use the A.L.R.3d & 4th Quick Index. Cite an A.L.R. annotation dealing with the presence of an alternate juror in a jury room as grounds for the reversal of a criminal conviction.
ANSWER:

Locate and examine the annotation to answer Questions 2 through 6.

2.   Does it cover the presence of an alternate juror as grounds for a mistrial?
ANSWER:

3.   Cite a Kentucky opinion in which the court reversed a conviction.
ANSWER:

4.   To which sections of the Am. Jur. 2d topic Jury could you turn to find related material?
ANSWER:

5.   State the name of the opinion whose text is printed in full.
ANSWER:

6.   Examine the Practice Pointers. State the name of a Florida opinion which held that a defendant cannot waive an error resulting from the presence of an alternate juror in the jury room.
ANSWER:

7. Use the Federal Quick Index. Cite an A.L.R. Fed. annotation dealing with the judicial review of Interior Department decisions affecting claims of mineral interests in public lands.
   ANSWER:

8. Find the annotation. Which section discusses discretionary action?
   ANSWER:

9. State the name of a <u>later</u> case (published after the annotation was written) from the 10th Circuit that updates the section in Question 8.
   ANSWER:

10. Have the following annotations been superseded? If so, cite the superseding annotation.

    168 A.L.R. 685   **ANSWER:**

    169 A.L.R. 290   **ANSWER:**

    53 A.L.R.3d 1285   **ANSWER:**

    1 A.L.R. Fed. 965   **ANSWER:**

11. Assume you have been reading the annotation at 19 A.L.R.2d 789 and want to find a more current Kentucky opinion relevant to § 4 of the annotation. Find it and state its name.
ANSWER:

12. Assume you have been reading the annotation at 70 A.L.R. 733-740 and want to find a relevant Illinois decision published between 1959 and 1967. Find it and state its name.
ANSWER:

13. The following decisions have been reported somewhere in the A.L.R. series. State the A.L.R. citation. (Use only A.L.R. and A.L.R. Fed. titles to answer this question.) (NOTE: you will find each answer in a different volume.)

Re Szaczywka's Estate   **ANSWER:**

Frkovich v. Petranovich   **ANSWER:**

Zapico v. Bucyrus-Erie Co.   **ANSWER:**

Abdallah v. Abdallah   **ANSWER:**

14. Answer this question from the knowledge you should have gained while studying A.L.R. The indexes will not be useful to you. If you were seeking an annotation published in the 1950s on federal Indian law, in which A.L.R. series would you expect to find it?
ANSWER:

GOALS: 1) To give you practice at using the A.L.R. indexes.
2) To make you familiar with parts of an annotation and the kinds of information regularly available in annotations.
3) To enable you to determine the current status of an annotation.
4) To enable you to find later cases relevant to an annotation.
5) To show you how to determine whether particular opinions have been printed in A.L.R.

In this assignment you will be using various volumes of American Law Reports (A.L.R.) and American Law Reports—Federal (A.L.R. Fed.). "Cite" means to give all available information in the correct format, but not to seek any information not given you by the A.L.R. citation.

1. Use the A.L.R.3d & 4th Quick Index. Cite an A.L.R. annotation dealing with the liability to pay for allegedly unauthorized repairs on a motor vehicle.
   ANSWER:

Locate and examine the annotation to answer Questions 2 through 6.

2. Does it cover in detail state statutory law?
   ANSWER:

3. Are any Idaho decisions mentioned in the annotation? If so, state their names.
   ANSWER:

4. To which sections of the Am. Jur. 2d topic Restitution and Implied Contracts could you turn to find related material?
   ANSWER:

5. State the name of the opinion whose text is printed in full.
   ANSWER:

6. Examine the Practice Pointers. Are any pointers offered to counsel for a mechanic?
   ANSWER:

7. Use the Federal Quick Index. Cite an A.L.R. Fed. annotation dealing with discharge from the armed forces on the grounds of conscientious objection.
   ANSWER:

8. Find the annotation. Which section generally discusses habeas corpus jurisdiction to review the denial of a discharge?
   ANSWER:

9. State the name of a <u>later</u> case (published after the annotation was printed) from the 4th Circuit that updates the section from Question 8.
   ANSWER:

10. Have the following annotations been superseded? If so, cite the superseding annotation.

    120 A.L.R. 535   **ANSWER:**

    29 A.L.R.3d 1021   **ANSWER:**

    149 A.L.R. 312   **ANSWER:**

    21 A.L.R. Fed. 708   **ANSWER:**

11. Assume you have been reading the annotation at 17 A.L.R.2d 1183 and want to find a more current South Dakota case for § 2 of the annotation. Find it and state its name.
ANSWER:

12. Assume you have been reading the annotation at 28 A.L.R. 1222-1230 and want to find a relevant Montana case published between 1968 and 1975. Find it and state its name.
ANSWER:

13. The following decisions have been reported somewhere in the A.L.R. series. State the A.L.R. citation. (Use only A.L.R. and A.L.R. Fed. titles to answer this question.) (NOTE: you will find each answer in a different volume.)

Lutfy v. United States   **ANSWER:**

Hare v. Winfree   **ANSWER:**

Voyager 1000 v. Civil Aeronautics
   Board   **ANSWER:**

Babe, Inc. v. Baby's Formula   **ANSWER:**
   Service, Inc.

14. Answer this question from the knowledge you should have gained while studying A.L.R. The indexes will not be useful to you. If you were seeking an annotation published in 1966 on federal tax law, in which A.L.R. series would you expect to find it?
ANSWER:

ASSIGNMENT IX
AMERICAN LAW REPORTS
EXERCISE D

GOALS:
1) To give you practice at using the A.L.R. indexes.
2) To make you familiar with parts of an annotation and the kinds of information regularly available in annotations.
3) To enable you to determine the current status of an annotation.
4) To enable you to find later cases relevant to an annotation.
5) To show you how to determine whether particular opinions have been printed in A.L.R.

In this assignment you will be using various volumes of American Law Reports (A.L.R.) and American Law Reports—Federal (A.L.R. Fed.). "Cite" means to give all available information in the correct format, but not to seek any information not given you by the A.L.R. citation.

1. Use the A.L.R.3d and 4th Quick Index. Cite an A.L.R. annotation dealing with whether or not farmers are "merchants" under Uniform Commercial Code Article 2.
ANSWER:

Locate and examine the annotation to answer Questions 2 through 6.

2. Cite a related A.L.R. annotation dealing with an implied warranty of fitness on the sale of livestock.
ANSWER:

3. Cite a Missouri appellate opinion holding that a soybean farmer was a merchant.
ANSWER:

4. To which sections of the U.S. Supreme Court Digest--Lawyers' Ed. topic Sale could you turn to find related material?
ANSWER:

5. State the name of the opinion whose text is printed in full.
ANSWER:

6. Examine the Practice Pointers. Do any of them mention the case you cited in Question 5?
ANSWER:

7. Use the Federal Quick Index. Cite an A.L.R. Fed. annotation dealing with the propriety of a federal judge's overruling or reconsidering a decision or order previously made in the same case by another district judge.
   ANSWER:

8. Find the annotation. Which section discusses the availability of the first judge?
   ANSWER:

9. State the name of a <u>later</u> case (published after the annotation was printed) from the 7th Circuit that updates the section in Question 8.
   ANSWER:

10. Have the following annotations been superseded? If so, cite the superseding annotation:

    169 A.L.R. 727   **ANSWER:**

    17 A.L.R. Fed. 522   **ANSWER:**

    156 A.L.R. 233   **ANSWER:**

    62 A.L.R.2d 1175   **ANSWER:**

11. Assume you have been reading the annotation at 9 A.L.R.2d 1026-1030 and want to find a more current Idaho case for § 2 of the annotation. Find it and state its name.
ANSWER:

12. Assume you have been reading the annotation at 76 A.L.R. 284-296 and want to find relevant Washington cases published before 1946. Find one and state its name.
ANSWER:

13. The following decisions have been reported somewhere in the A.L.R. series. State the A.L.R. citation. (Use only A.L.R. and A.L.R. Fed. titles to answer this question.) (NOTE: you will find each answer in a different volume.)

Leclerc v. Leclerc   **ANSWER:**

Stifel v. Hopkins   **ANSWER:**

Bool v. Bool   **ANSWER:**

DeZort v. Hinsdale   **ANSWER:**

14. Answer this question from the knowledge you should have gained while studying A.L.R. The indexes will not be useful to you. If you were seeking an annotation published in the 1950s on federal labor law, in which A.L.R. series would you expect to find it?
ANSWER:

INTRODUCTION
TO CHAPTER X
FEDERAL SESSION LAWS

The following assignment is intended to acquaint you with federal session laws. Federal session laws are published in official form in the United States Statutes at Large (Stat.) In Stat. you will simply find the text of all laws as they are passed by Congress, in chronological order. Another source of session laws is the United States Code Congressional and Administrative News, published by West. It is cited as U.S. Code Cong. & Ad. News, although you will sometimes see it referred to as U.S.C.C.A.N. It is an unofficial source of session laws and is updated by monthly pamphlets. If you are seeking a recent session law you may wish to check U.S. Code Cong. & Ad. News first, although you should also check other sources, such as the CCH commercial slip law service and the United States Code Service pamphlets, which contain new laws in session law form. U.S. Code Cong. & Ad. News also contains texts or excerpts of Congressional reports on bills which have become law. Such reports are a valuable source of legislative history.

Before beginning this assignment, read the pertinent sections of Chapter 7, "Statutes and Related Material," of Cohen and Berring, How to Find the Law, 8th ed.

ASSIGNMENT X
FEDERAL SESSION LAWS
EXERCISE B

GOALS: 1) To introduce you to federal session laws as they appear in United States Statutes at Large and to enable you to find them therein.

2) To teach you how to use various finding aids and tables in the United States Code Congressional and Administrative News, so that you will know how to determine a United States Code (U.S.C.) citation for a section of a session law or so that you can discover whether language in the U.S.C. has been modified or repealed.

To answer Questions 1-5, use volume 93 of United States Statutes at Large.

1. On what page does the Archaeological Resources Protection Act of 1979 begin?
   ANSWER:

2. What is the public law number of the act?
   ANSWER:

3. What was the bill number of the act?
   ANSWER:

4. On what date was the act signed into law?
   ANSWER:

5. State the United States Code citation for Section 12 of the act.
   ANSWER:

To answer Questions 6-10, use the tables volume of the 1979 United States Code Congressional and Administrative News (U.S. Code Cong. & Ad. News).

6. Use the index. Beginning on what page of the 1979 U.S. Cong. & Ad. News could you find legislative history for the Archaeological Resources Protection Act of 1979?
   ANSWER:

7. Look up the legislative history from Question 6. Which Congressional publication from the act's history is set out here?
   ANSWER:

8. Using the appropriate table, tell which title and section of the U.S.C. corresponds to Section 1(a) of P.L. 96-71.
   ANSWER:

9. Using the appropriate table, tell on which page of 93 Stat. a statute can be found which amends or repeals 45 U.S.C. § 545(i).
   ANSWER:

10. Using the appropriate table, tell on which page of 93 Stat. the Walsh-Healey Act amendment begins.
    ANSWER:

ASSIGNMENT X
FEDERAL SESSION LAWS
EXERCISE C

GOALS: 1) To introduce you to federal session laws as they appear in United States Statutes at Large and to enable you to find them therein.

2) To teach you how to use various finding aids and tables in the United States Code Congressional and Administrative News, so that you will know how to determine a United States Code (U.S.C.) citation for a section of a session law or so that you can discover whether language in the U.S.C. has been modified or repealed.

To answer Questions 1-5, use volume 92 of United States Statutes at Large.

1. On what page does the Airline Deregulation Act of 1978 begin?
ANSWER:

2. What is the public law number of the act?
ANSWER:

3. What was the bill number of the act?
ANSWER:

4. On what date was the act signed into law?
ANSWER:

5. State the United States Code citation for Section 39 of the act.
ANSWER:

To answer Questions 6-10, use the tables volume of the 1978 United States Code Congressional and Administrative News (U.S. Code Cong. & Ad. News).

6. Use the index. Beginning on what page of the 1978 U.S. Cong. & Ad. News can you find legislative history for the Airline Deregulation Act of 1978?
ANSWER:

7. Look up the legislative history from Question 6. Which Congressional publications from the act's history are set out here?
    ANSWER:

8. Using the appropriate table, tell which title and section of the U.S.C. corresponds to Section 22 of the Airline Deregulation Act of 1978.
    ANSWER:

9. Using the appropriate table, tell on which page of 92 Stat. a statute can be found which amends or repeals 31 U.S.C. § 68d.
    ANSWER:

10. Using the appropriate table, tell on which page of 92 Stat. the Sikes Act amendment begins.
    ANSWER:

GOALS: 1) To introduce you to federal session laws as they appear in United States Statutes at Large and to enable you to find them therein.
2) To teach you how to use various finding aids and tables in the United States Code Congressional and Administrative News, so that you will know how to determine a United States Code (U.S.C.) citation for a section of a session law or so that you can discover whether language in the U.S.C. has been modified or repealed.

To answer Questions 1-5, use volume 91 of United States Statutes at Large.

1. On what page does the Earthquake Hazards Reduction Act of 1977 begin?
   ANSWER:

2. What is the public law number of the act?
   ANSWER:

3. What was the bill number of the act?
   ANSWER:

4. On what date was the act signed into law?
   ANSWER:

5. State the United States Code citation for Section 4 of the act.
   ANSWER:

To answer Questions 6-10, use the tables volume of the 1977 United States Code Congressional and Administrative News (U.S. Code Cong. & Ad. News).

6. Use the index. Beginning on what page of the 1977 U.S. Cong. & Ad. News could you find legislative history for the Earthquake Hazards Reduction Act of 1977?
   ANSWER:

7. Look up the legislative history from Question 6. Which Congressional publication from the act's history is set out here?
    ANSWER:

8. Using the appropriate table, tell which title and section of the U.S.C. corresponds to Section 111 of P.L. 95-26.
    ANSWER:

9. Using the appropriate table, tell on which page of 91 Stat. a statute can be found which amends or repeals 26 U.S.C. § 51.
    ANSWER:

10. Using the appropriate table, tell on which page of 91 Stat. the Bankhead-Jones Act amendment begins.
    ANSWER:

INTRODUCTION
TO CHAPTER XI
UNITED STATES CODES

This assignment will require you to use the official code of federal statutes entitled the United States Code, and the two unofficial annotated codes, the United States Code Annotated and United States Code Service. All three of the codes use the same numbering system, so there is no need to convert from unofficial to official citation, as there is with published cases. The unofficial codes have several advantages: they are published more quickly, so are more current, and they contain various additional materials, such as historical notes, cross references to the Code of Federal Regulations, and case annotations. Case annotations, as opposed to A.L.R. annotations, are headnotes from court decisions which interpret the statutes.

This exercise will require you to draw conclusions as to the similiarities and differences among the codes, and disadvantages and advantages of using one over the others in particular situations. Before beginning this assignment, read about the three codes in Chapter 7, "Statutes and Related Materials," in How to Find the Law, 8th ed.

ASSIGNMENT XI
UNITED STATES CODES
EXERCISE B

GOALS: 1) To require you to use the official <u>United States Code</u> (U.S.C.) and the two unofficial annotated codes and to discover the differences between official and unofficial codes in general, by contrasting the format and availability of current statutory text, the availability of case annotations, and the kinds of supplementary references and indexes.

2) To require you to become acquainted with the differences between the <u>United States Code Annotated</u> (U.S.C.A.) and the <u>United States Code Service</u> (U.S.C.S.), by using the features and tables of each.

1. Using the <u>United States Code</u>, the <u>United States Code Annotated</u>, or the <u>United States Code Service</u>, cite the title and section of the Code dealing with the escape of prisoners in the custody of an institution or officer.
ANSWER:

To answer Questions 2-9, use all three code versions of the section you found in Question 1.

2. State the date, public law number, and <u>U.S. Statutes at Large</u> reference for the most recent amendment to this section.
ANSWER:

3. In which of the codes could you find the answer to Question 2?
ANSWER:

4. One of the codes refers you to a relevant West topic and key numbers.

a. Which code does so?
ANSWER:

b. What are the topic and key numbers?
ANSWER:

5. Which code refers you to Am. Jur. 2d?
   ANSWER:

6. Which codes refer you to relevant court decisions?
   ANSWER:

7. State the name of a 1973 case found in the case annotations for this section concerning escape from a halfway house.
   ANSWER:

8. One of the codes cites a relevant section of the <u>Code of Federal Regulations.</u>

   a. Which code does so?
       ANSWER:

   b. What is the citation?
       ANSWER:

9. Which code refers to a relevant law review article?
   ANSWER:

10. Using the Popular Name Table in any one of the three code versions, state the citation of the Mixed Flour Act as it appears in the table (you may find that not every service contains it).
    ANSWER:

11. Using the appropriate table in <u>any</u> of the three code versions, state the <u>United States Code</u> title and section that corresponds to:

    a.   P.L. 85-315, Sec. 104   **ANSWER:**

    b.   45 Stat. 1224, Sec. 8   **ANSWER:**

12. Assume you have a citation to Sec. 14 of <u>old</u> Title 3 of the U.S.C. You know that Title 3 was revised in 1948. Using the appropriate table, state the corresponding new title and section number.
    ANSWER:

13. Examine the current pamphlet supplements for the two unofficial codes. Which is published in session law, as opposed to code, form?
    ANSWER:

14. Examine the two unofficial code versions. In which could you find the rules of procedure for administrative agencies?
    ANSWER:

15. Has 4 U.S.C. been enacted into positive law?
    ANSWER:

16. Assume you have a citation to Section 4294 of the <u>United States Revised Statutes.</u> Using the appropriate table, tell where it <u>can be found in the U.S. Code.</u>
    ANSWER:

GOALS: 1) To require you to use the official United States Code (U.S.C.) and
the two unofficial annotated codes and to discover the differences
between official and unofficial codes in general, by contrasting the
format and availability of current statutory text, the availability
of case annotations, and the kinds of supplementary references and
indexes.

2) To require you to become acquainted with the differences between
the United States Code Annotated (U.S.C.A.) and the United States
Code Service (U.S.C.S.), by using the features and tables of each.

1. Using the United States Code, the United States Code Annotated, or the
United States Code Service, cite the title and section of the Code dealing
with fair use as a limitation on the exclusive rights of the owner of a
copyright, as found in the 1976 Copyright Act.
ANSWER:

To answer Questions 2-9, use all three code versions of the section you found
in Question 1.

2. State the date, public law number, and U.S. Statutes at Large reference for
the section.
ANSWER:

3. In which of the three codes could you find the answer to Question 2?
ANSWER:

4. One of the codes refers you to a relevant West topic and key numbers.

a. Which code does so?
ANSWER:

b. What are the topic and key numbers?
ANSWER:

5. Which code refers you to a relevant A.L.R 3d annotation?
ANSWER:

6. Which codes refer you to relevant court decisions?
ANSWER:

7. State the name of a 1975 court case found in the case annotations for this section holding that the playing of the "Mickey Mouse March" to accompany a sex scene in a movie was not fair use.
ANSWER:

8. One of the codes cites a relevant section of the Code of Federal Regulations.

   a. Which code does so?
   ANSWER:

   b. What is the citation?
   ANSWER:

9. Which code contains excerpts from the House Report on the Copyright Bill?
ANSWER:

10. Using the Popular Name Table in any one of the three code versions, state the citation of the Blue Star Mothers of America Act as it appears in the table (you may find that not every service contains it).
ANSWER:

11. Using the appropriate table in <u>any</u> of the three code versions, state the
    <u>United States Code</u> title and section that corresponds to:

    a.   86 Stat. 14, Sec. 303   **ANSWER:**

    b.   P.L. 86-778, Sec. 542(d)   **ANSWER:**

12. Assume you have a citation to Sec. 292c-1 of <u>old</u> Title 10 of the U.S.C.
    You know that Title 10 was revised in 1956. Using the appropriate table,
    state the corresponding new title and section number.
    ANSWER:

13. Examine the current pamphlet supplements for the two unofficial codes.
    Which is published in session law, as opposed to code, form?
    ANSWER:

14. Examine the two unofficial code versions. In which could you find annotations
    to selected <u>uncodified</u> federal laws and treaties?
    ANSWER:

15. Has 10 U.S.C. been enacted into positive law?
    ANSWER:

16. Assume you have a citation to Section 5590 of the <u>United States Revised
    Statutes.</u> Using the appropriate table, tell where it can be found in the
    <u>U.S. Code.</u>
    ANSWER:

GOALS: 1)   To require you to use the official United States Code (U.S.C.) and the two unofficial annotated codes and to discover the differences between official and unofficial codes in general, by contrasting the format and availability of current statutory text, the availability of case annotations, and the kinds of supplementary references and indexes.

2)   To require you to become acquainted with the differences between the United States Code Annotated (U.S.C.A.) and the United States Code Service (U.S.C.S.), by using the features and tables of each.

1. Using the United States Code, the United States Code Annotated, or the United States Code Service, cite the title and section of the Code dealing with consent to grant rights of way through Indian lands and reservations.
   ANSWER:

To answer Questions 2-9, use all three code versions of the section you found in Question 1.

2. State the date and U.S. Statutes at Large reference to this section.
   ANSWER:

3. In which of the three codes could you find the answer to Question 2?
   ANSWER:

4. One of the codes refers you to a relevant West topic and key number.

   a.   Which code does so?
   ANSWER:

   b.   What are the topic and key number?
   ANSWER:

5. Which code refers you to Am. Jur. 2d?
   ANSWER:

6. Which code refers you to relevant court decisions?
   ANSWER:

7. State the name of a case found in the case annotations for this section involving the jurisdiction of the tribal court.
   ANSWER:

8. Two of the codes cite a relevant section of the Code of Federal Regulations.

   a. Which codes do so?
      ANSWER:

   b. What are the citations?
      ANSWER:

9. In what other title of the U.S. Code can you find a reference to this section?
   ANSWER:

10. Using the Popular Name Table in any one of the three code versions, state the citation of the Ash Pan Act as it appears in the table (you may find that not every service contains it).
    ANSWER:

11. Using the appropriate table in <u>any</u> of the three code versions, state the <u>United States Code</u> title and section that corresponds to:

    a. 84 Stat. 202, Sec. 2   **ANSWER:**

    b. P.L. 87-195, Sec. 204   **ANSWER:**

12. Assume you have a citation to Sec. 126 of <u>old</u> Title 28 of the U.S.C. You know that Title 28 was revised in 1948. Using the appropriate table, state the corresponding new title and section number.
    ANSWER:

13. Examine the current pamphlet supplements for the two unofficial codes. Which is published in session law, as opposed to code, form?
    ANSWER:

14. Examine the two unofficial code versions. In which could you find the text of executive orders in the pamphlet supplements?
    ANSWER:

15. Has 9 U.S.C. been enacted into positive law?
    ANSWER:

16. Assume you have a citation to Section 5236 of the <u>United States Revised Statutes.</u> Using the appropriate table, tell where it can be found in the <u>U.S. Code.</u>
    ANSWER:

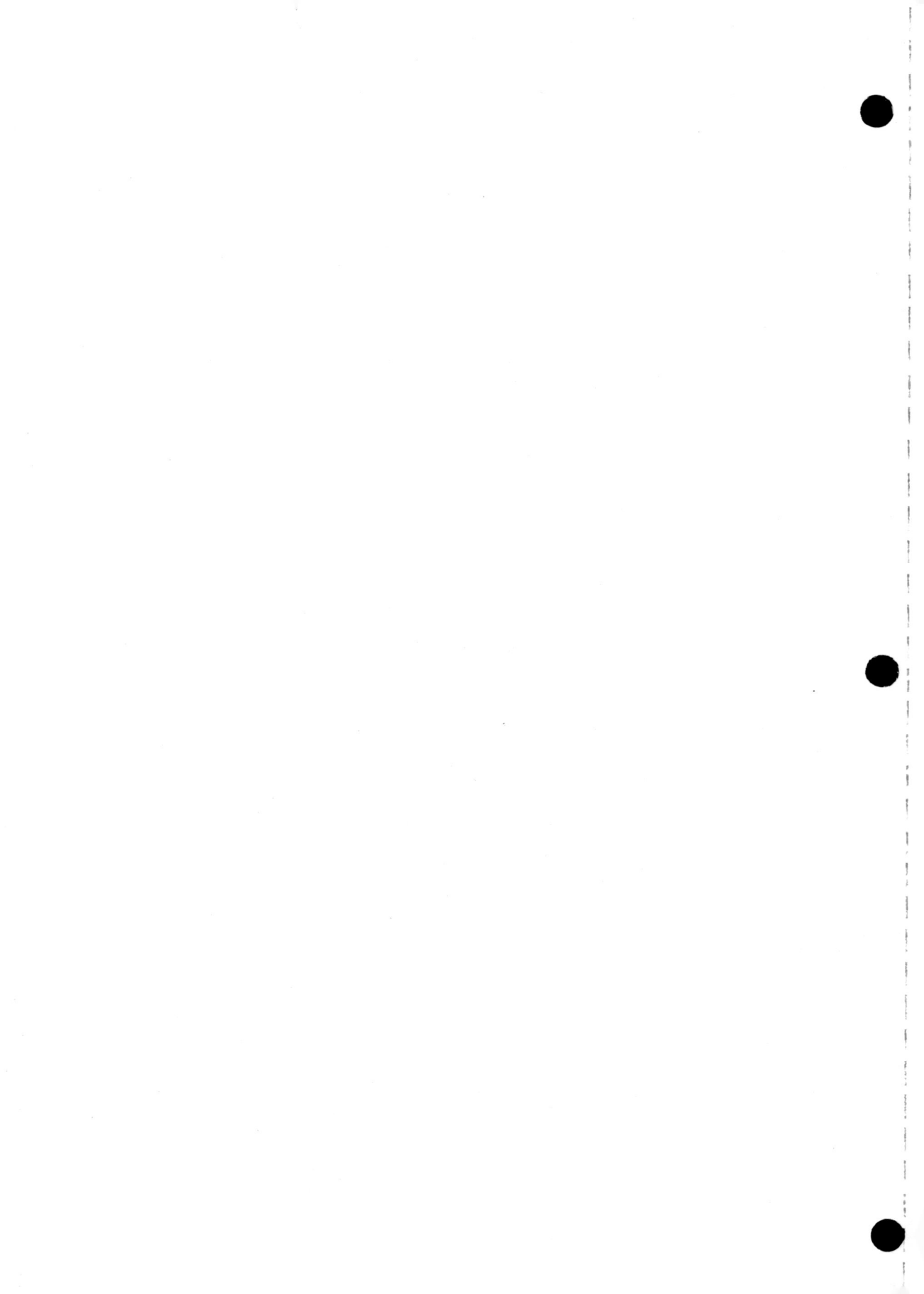

INTRODUCTION
TO CHAPTER XII
COURT RULES

This exercise will acquaint you with various materials concerning court rules. Before beginning this assignment, read Chapter 8, "Court Rules," in Cohen and Berring, <u>How to Find the Law</u>, 8th ed.

For the first part of the assignment, you will find a federal court rule in the <u>United States Code</u>, the <u>United States Code Annotated</u>, and the <u>United States Code Service.</u> Court rules can sometimes be found at the same location in each code version, but not always. Below is a guide:

Federal Rules of Civil Procedure
U.S.C. and U.S.C.A. .... Title 28 Appendix
U.S.C.S. .... End of Set

Federal Rules of Criminal Procedure
U.S.C. and U.S.C.A. .... Title 18 Appendix
U.S.C.S. .... End of Set

Federal Rules of Appellate Procedure
U.S.C. and U.S.C.A. .... Title 28 Appendix
U.S.C.S. .... End of Set

Federal Rules of Evidence
U.S.C., U.S.C.A. and U.S.C.S. .... Title 28 Appendix

Rules of practice for administrative agencies can be found in the <u>Code of Federal Regulations</u>, but they are also conveniently gathered together in three volumes of U.S.C.S. You will be required to find such a rule, using U.S.C.S.

Rules of the individual U.S. district courts, as well as other procedural materials, can be found in Callaghan's <u>Federal Rules Service</u>, which you will use to answer several questions. Finally, treatises of an encyclopedic nature have been written about the various federal procedural rules. You will be required to consult one such treatise.

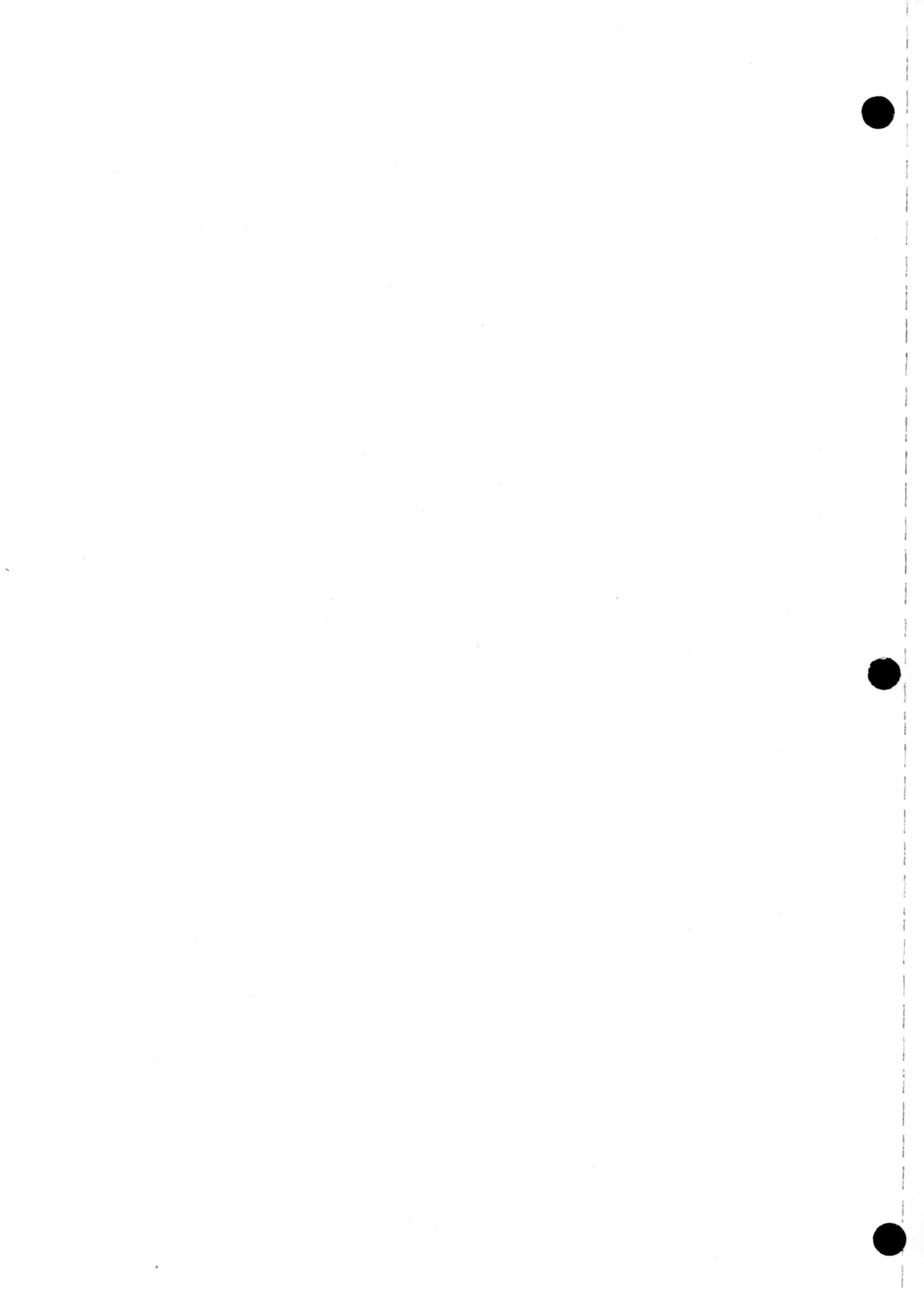

      c.   Can you find cases interpreting the Federal Rules of Civil and Appellate Procedure in this service?
ANSWER:

      d.   List the volume and page number of the <u>Federal Rules Service</u> where the full text of <u>Diaz v. San Nicolas</u> appears.
ANSWER:

9.   Use <u>Federal Procedure, Lawyers Edition</u> to answer the following questions.

      a.   Generally, will grossly offensive unethical conduct on the part of counsel for a class action affect the certification of the class?
ANSWER:

      b.   State the section where you found the answer.
ANSWER:

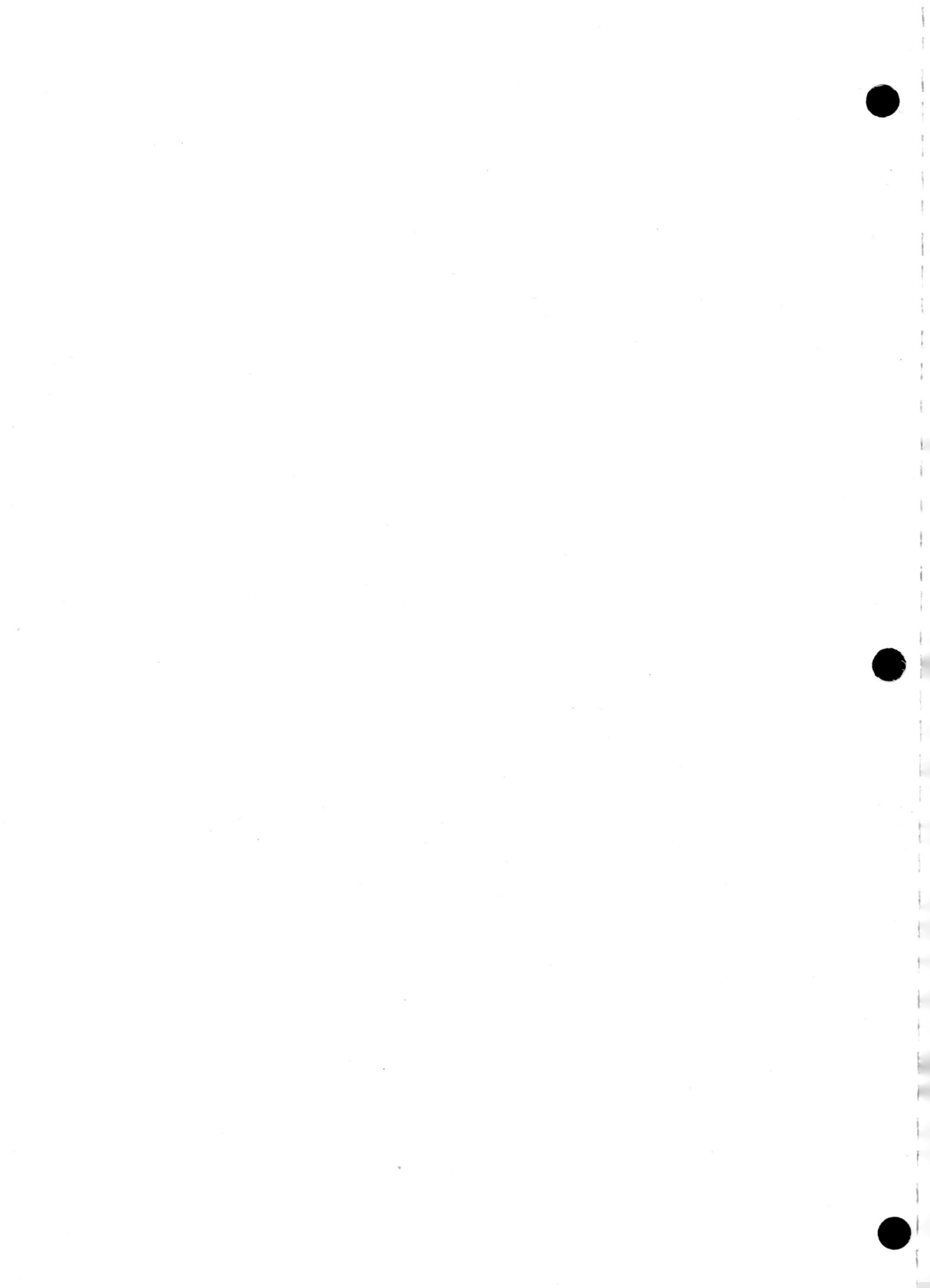

ASSIGNMENT XII
COURT RULES
EXERCISE B

GOALS: 1) To familiarize you with the process of finding federal court rules in the three versions of the United States Code.
2) To acquaint you with rules of practice for federal administrative agencies and give you practice at locating them.
3) To introduce you to one of the leading treatises on federal court rules.
4) To orient you to the process of finding federal district court rules.

To answer Questions 1-3, use the United States Code, the United States Code Annotated, and the United States Code Service.

1. Which Federal Rule of Evidence concerns judicial notice?
ANSWER:

Find the rule and examine the information provided by the three code versions to answer Questions 2 and 3. Only one will contain each answer.

2. List the pertinent Federal Rules of Civil Procedure which correspond most closely with the rule in Question 1.
ANSWER:

3. State the title of the law review discussing the rule in Question 1 that was published in the University of Florida Law Review.
ANSWER:

Use the Federal Rules of Appellate Procedure in any one of the three code versions to answer Questions 4 and 5.

4. In a criminal case, how soon after the entry of judgment must the defendant file a notice of appeal with the district court?
ANSWER:

5. How many copies must be filed of a petition to appeal in a bankruptcy case?
    ANSWER:

6. Use the U.S.C.S. volume titled Administrative Rules of Procedure which contains the Federal Communication Commission's rules. To practice before the FCC, does an attorney have to be admitted to practice before federal courts?
    ANSWER:

Use Callaghan's <u>Federal Rules Service</u> to answer Questions 7 and 8.

7. Use the Federal Local Court Rules volumes. Find the rules of the U.S. District Court for the District of North Dakota. Does a magistrate appointed by the court have the power to conduct extradition proceedings?
    ANSWER:

8. Use the Finding Aids volume. Read "How to Use this Service" and answer the following questions.

    a. If you are seeking cases on the Federal Rules of Criminal Procedure should you use this service?
        ANSWER:

    b. Can you find the full text of the Federal Rules of Evidence in this service?
        ANSWER:

    c.   Can you find cases interpreting the Federal Rules of Civil and Appellate Procedure in this service?
ANSWER:

    d.   List the volume and page number of the Federal Rules Service where the full text of Hassenflu v. Pyke appears.
ANSWER:

9.   Use Federal Procedure, Lawyer's Edition to answer the following questions.

    a.   In a federal civil trial, may the jury consist of fewer than twelve members?
ANSWER:

    b.   State the section where you found the answer.
ANSWER:

GOALS: 1) To familiarize you with the process of finding federal court rules in the three versions of the United States Code.
2) To acquaint you with rules of practice for federal administrative agencies and give you practice at locating them.
3) To introduce you to one of the leading treatises on federal court rules.
4) To orient you to the process of finding federal district court rules.

To answer Questions 1-3, use the United States Code, the United States Code Annotated, and the United States Code Service.

1. Which Federal Rule of Criminal Procedure concerns the jury verdict?
    ANSWER:

Find the rule and examine the information provided by the three code versions to answer Questions 2 and 3. Only one will contain each answer.

2. To which topic and section of Wright and Miller's Federal Practice and Procedure would you refer to read about the verdict?
    ANSWER:

3. State the title of the law review article concerning inconsistent verdicts.
    ANSWER:

Use the Federal Rules of Appellate Procedure in any one of the three code versions to answer Questions 4 and 5.

4. If a party wishes to appeal a district court judgment in forma pauperis, where must the party file a motion for leave to so proceed?
    ANSWER:

5. When a party is applying for an extraordinary writ of mandamus, what must be filed with the clerk of the court of appeals?
    ANSWER:

6. Use the U.S.C.S. volume titled Administrative Rules of Procedure which contains the Interstate Commerce Commission's rules. May non-attorneys practice before the ICC?
    ANSWER:

Use Callaghan's <u>Federal Rules Service</u> to answer Questions 7 and 8.

7. Use the Federal Local Court Rules volumes. Find the rules of the U.S. District Court for the Eastern District of Washington. May an attorney residing in and licensed to practice only in Indiana obtain permission from the court to appear as sole counsel for a party?
    ANSWER:

8. Use the Finding Aids volume. Read "How to Use this Service" and answer the following questions.

    a. If you are seeking cases on the Federal Rules of Criminal Procedure should you use this service?
        ANSWER:

    b. Can you find the full text of the Federal Rules of Evidence in this service?
        ANSWER:

      c.   Can you find cases interpreting the Federal Rules of Civil and Appellate Procedure in this service?
ANSWER:

      d.   List the volume and page number of the Federal Rules Service where the full text of Jaroslawicz v. Seedman appears.
ANSWER:

9.   Use Wright and Miller, Federal Practice and Procedure.

      a.   Assume you are interested in whether Federal Rule of Civil Procedure 6(a) is applicable to federal statutes of limitation. What is the majority rule?
ANSWER:

      b.   State the section where you found the answer.
ANSWER:

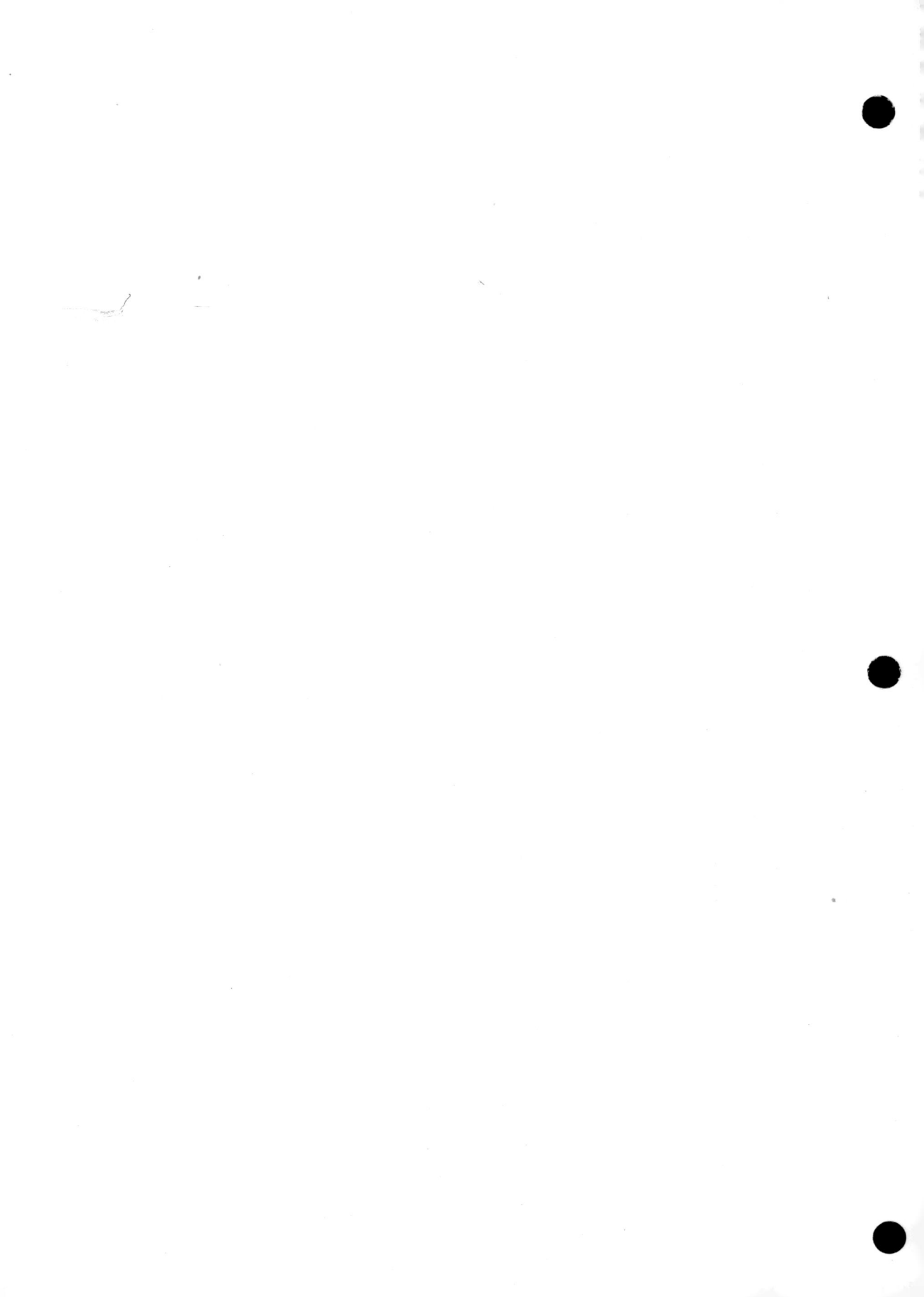

ASSIGNMENT XII
COURT RULES
EXERCISE D

GOALS: 1) To familiarize you with the process of finding federal court rules in the three versions of the United States Code.
2) To acquaint you with rules of practice for federal administrative agencies and give you practice at locating them.
3) To introduce you to one of the leading treatises on federal court rules.
4) To orient you to the process of finding federal district court rules.

To answer Questions 1-3, use the United States Code, the United States Code Annotated, and the United States Code Service.

1. Which Federal Rule of Evidence concerns the admissibility of relevant evidence?
ANSWER:

Find the rule and examine the information provided by the three code versions to answer Questions 2 and 3. Only one will contain each answer.

2. List the pertinent Federal Rules of Civil Procedure which correspond most closely with the rule in Question 1.
ANSWER:

3. State the title of the article discussing the rule in Question 1 that was published in 55 Harvard Law Review.
ANSWER:

Use the Federal Rules of Appellate Procedure in any one of the three code versions to answer Questions 4 and 5.

4. May a party file a response in opposition to a motion other than one for a procedural order?
ANSWER:

5. What is the deadline for serving and filing of the appellant's brief?
    ANSWER:

6. Use the U.S.C.S. volume titled Administrative Rules of Procedure which
    contains the Immigration and Naturalization Service's rules. Are exclusion
    hearings on aliens generally open to the public?
    ANSWER:

Use Callaghan's <u>Federal Rules Service</u> to answer Questions 7 and 8.

7. Use the Federal Local Court Rules volumes. Find the rules of the U.S.
    District Court for the Eastern District of Tennessee. Is there a special
    day set aside by the court for the arguing of motions?
    ANSWER:

8. Use the Finding Aids volume. Read "How to Use this Service" and answer
    the following questions.

    a. If you are seeking cases on the Federal Rules of Criminal Procedure
        should you use this service?
        ANSWER:

    b. Can you find the full text of the Federal Rules of Evidence in
        this service?
        ANSWER:

        c.   Can you find cases interpreting the Federal Rules of Civil and Appellate Procedure in this service?
ANSWER:

        d.   List the volume and page number of the Federal Rules Service where the full text of Oquendo v. Monsanto Co. appears.
ANSWER:

9.   Use Wright and Miller, Federal Practice and Procedure.

        a.   Assume you are interested in whether under Federal Rule of Civil Procedure 49 state law usually controls the submission of special verdicts and interrogatories. Does it?
ANSWER:

        b.   State the section where you found the answer.
ANSWER:

INTRODUCTION
TO CHAPTER XIII
SHEPARD'S CITATORS—CASES

The following assignment will give you experience in Shepardizing cases. All Shepard's are basically similar, but no two are completely alike. In this assignment you will use the Shepard's covering U.S. Supreme Court cases, a state Shepard's, and the corresponding regional Shepard's.

Remember when Shepardizing that it is almost always necessary to check more than a bound volume. Bound volumes were used in this assignment for the sake of accuracy of the answers.

Before beginning this assignment, read the relevant parts of Chapter 9, "Citators," in Cohen and Berring, How to Find the Law, 8th ed., and the pamphlet How to Use Shepard's Citations.

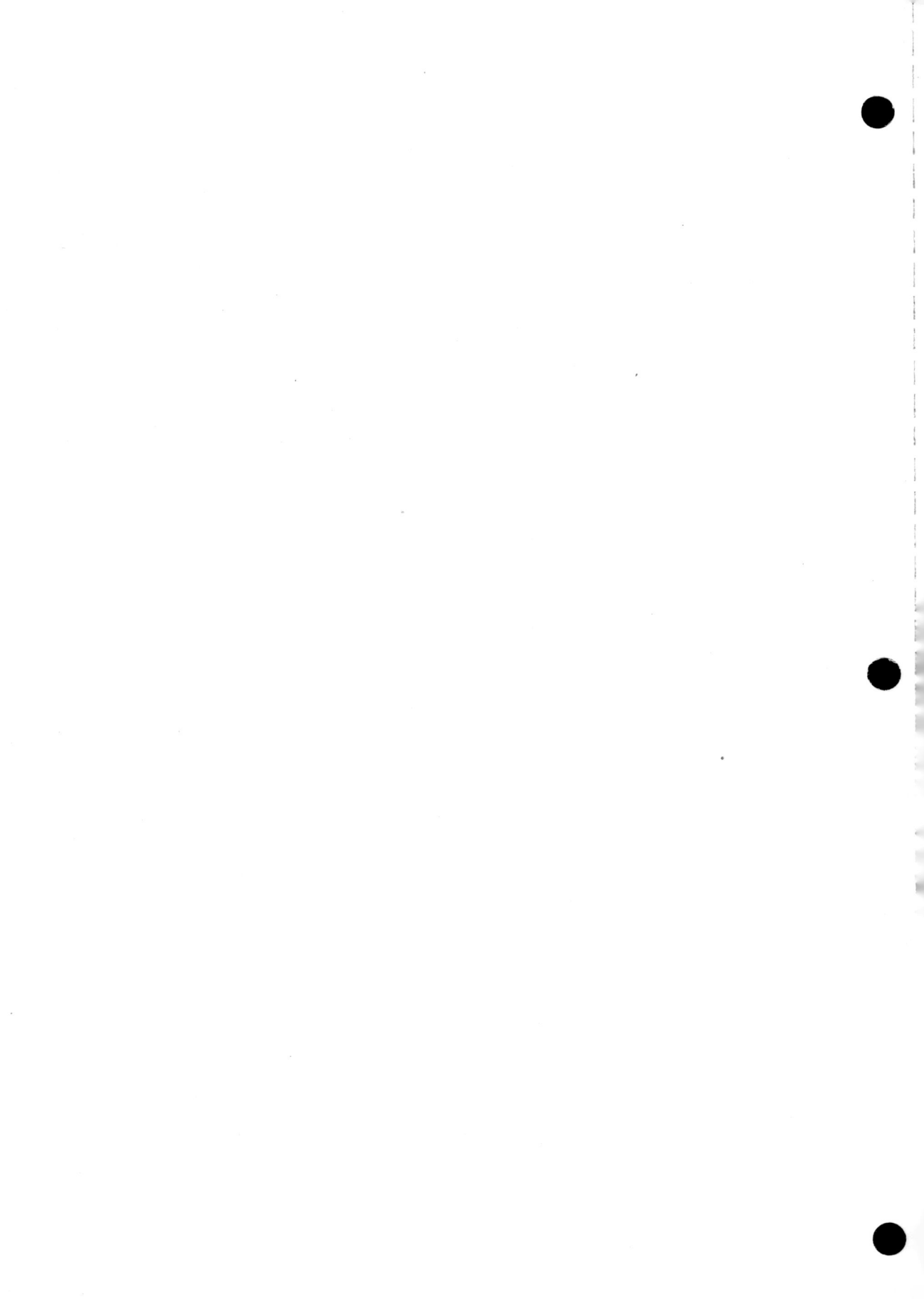

ASSIGNMENT XIII
SHEPARD'S CITATORS--CASES
EXERCISE B

GOALS: 1) To give you experience in Shepardizing court opinions, identifying the citing materials, and interpreting their treatment of the cited opinion.

2) To teach you how to use Shepard's to identify parallel citations for either official or unofficial court decisions.

3) To help you internalize the differences in scope of citing materials found in the various sections of Shepard's United States Citations--Cases and found in the Shepard's complementary state and regional reporters.

NOTE: When a case citation appears in your answers, use the standard abbreviation for the reporter as found in A Uniform System of Citation, 13th ed. It may differ substantially from the Shepard's abbreviation. If a law review citation is your answer, write out the title of the law review in full.

To answer Questions 1-4 use only the 1976-1980 Case Edition Supplement of Shepard's United States Citations--Cases (Vol. 5). First read pp. vii-xvii and the introduction to the U.S., L. Ed., and S. Ct. sections on pages 1, 649, and 1021. Note for each section the "citing" materials which have referred to the Supreme Court cases.

1. Using the U.S. section of this volume, state the parallel citations for 431 U.S. 767.
    ANSWER:

2. What is the official Illinois Supreme Court citation for this case (i.e., what is the citation to the same case in the immediate court below)?
    ANSWER:

3. What Oregon opinion cited 431 U.S. 767? Provide both the official and unofficial citations.
    ANSWER:

4. What opinion explained the decision in 431 U.S. 767? Provide the citation.
    ANSWER:

5. Find the case from Questions 1-4 under its L. Ed. citation in the L. Ed. section. What U.S. District Court opinion distinguished the decision?
   ANSWER:

6. Find the case from Questions 1-5 under its S. Ct. citation in the S. Ct. section. What U.S. District Court opinion cited a point of law from West headnote number 4 of the cited case?
   ANSWER:

Now you have examined entries of materials which cite one case in all three sections under each of its citations. Be sure to use the appropriate section when answering Questions 7-11.

7. State the citation of the A.L.R. annotation which cited 20 L. Ed. 2d 522.
   ANSWER:

8. Did the A.L.R. annotation reference to 20 L. Ed. 2d 522 in the previous question appear in the annotation or its supplement? (If you need help with this question, refer back to the last paragraph on p. xi.)
   ANSWER:

9. Find the entry for 60 S. Ct. 1. Why is no parallel citation listed?
   ANSWER:

10. State the citation of the annotation appearing in United States Supreme Court Reports—Lawyers' Edition which referred to 67 S. Ct. 544.
    ANSWER:

11. What opinion cited White's concurrence with 428 U.S. 242? Provide the citation.
    ANSWER:

12. Which of the three sections lists citing opinions from state courts?

_____ U.S.

_____ L. Ed.

_____ S. Ct.

13. Which of the three sections list citing A.L.R. Fed. annotations?

_____ U.S.

_____ L. Ed.

_____ S. Ct.

14. Which of the three sections lists citing opinions of selected administrative courts?

_____ U.S.

_____ L. Ed.

_____ S. Ct.

To answer Questions 15 and 16, use only the 1968-1980 Supplement to Shepard's New Jersey Citations and the 1978-1982 Supplement to Vol. 2 of Shepard's Atlantic Reporter Citations, Parts 1 and 2. First, read the introductions on pp. xii-1 and 311 of the New Jersey volume and pp. viii-1 of the Atlantic volume.

15. Find the entry for 75 N.J. 272. What is the parallel citation to the Atlantic Reporter?
ANSWER:

16. Additionally, locate the entry for the opinion under its <u>Atlantic</u> citation in the New Jersey Shepard's and the Atlantic Shepard's. Looking at the entries for this opinion in all <u>three</u> places, answer the following questions:

    a. Cite the law review article which refers to 75 N.J. 272. (Write out the name of the law review.)
       ANSWER:

    b. List the citation of the Nebraska opinion which cites 75 N.J. 272.
       ANSWER:

    c. What happened in the subsequent <u>history</u> (not treatment) of 75 N.J. 272 after the New Jersey Supreme Court rendered its decision?
       ANSWER:

17. When Shepardizing a particular citation, where will you find a complete list of the bound volumes and supplements you will need to check?
    ANSWER:

GOALS: 1) To give you experience in Shepardizing court opinions, identifying the citing materials, and interpreting their treatment of the cited opinion.

2) To teach you how to use Shepard's to identify parallel citations for either official or unofficial court decisions.

3) To help you internalize the differences in scope of citing materials found in the various sections of Shepard's United States Citations--Cases and found in the Shepard's complementary state and regional reporters.

NOTE: When a case citation appears in your answers, use the standard abbreviation for the reporter as found in A Uniform System of Citation, 13th ed. It may differ substantially from the Shepard's abbreviation. If a law review citation is your answer, write out the title of the law review in full.

To answer Questions 1-4 use only the 1980-1982 Case Edition Supplement of Shepard's United States Citations--Cases (Vol. 6). First read pp. vii-xvii and the introduction to the U.S., L. Ed., and S. Ct. sections on pages 1, 463, and 731. Note for each section the "citing" materials which have referred to the Supreme Court cases.

1. Using the U.S. section of this volume, state the parallel citations for 443 U.S. 157.
   ANSWER:

2. What is the U.S. Circuit Court of Appeals citation for this case (i.e., what is the citation to the same case in the immediate court below)?
   ANSWER:

3. What Maryland decision cited 443 U.S. 157? Provide both the official and unofficial citations.
   ANSWER:

4. What opinions explained the decision in 443 U.S. 157? Provide the citations.
   ANSWER:

5. Find the case from Questions 1-4 under its L. Ed. citation in the L. Ed. section. What U.S. District Court opinion distinguished the decision?
ANSWER:

6. Find the case from Questions 1-5 under its S. Ct. citation in the S. Ct. section. What opinion cited a point of law from West headnote number 5 of the cited case?
ANSWER:

Now you have examined entries of materials which cite one case in all three sections under each of its citations. Be sure to use the appropriate section when answering Questions 7-11.

7. State the citation of the A.L.R. annotation which cited 61 L. Ed. 2d 220.
ANSWER:

8. Did the A.L.R. annotation reference to 61 L. Ed. 2d 220 in the previous question appear in the annotation or its supplement? (If you need help with this question, refer back to the last paragraph on p. xi.)
ANSWER:

9. Find the entry for 68 S. Ct. 1375. Why is no parallel citation listed?
ANSWER:

10. State the citation of the annotation appearing in United States Supreme Court Reports—Lawyers' Edition which referred to 94 S. Ct. 1734.
ANSWER:

11. What U.S. District Court opinion cited Blackmun's dissent from 446 U.S. 55? Provide the citation.
ANSWER:

12. Which of the three sections lists citing opinions from state courts?

    _____   U.S.

    _____   L. Ed.

    _____   S. Ct.

13. Which of the three sections list citing A.L.R. Fed. annotations?

    _____   U.S.

    _____   L. Ed.

    _____   S. Ct.

14. Which of the three sections lists citing opinions of selected administrative courts?

    _____   U.S.

    _____   L. Ed.

    _____   S. Ct.

To answer Questions 15 and 16, use only the 1979 Case Edition of Shepard's Wisconsin Citations—Cases and the 1979 (Vol. 2) Edition of Shepard's Northwestern Reporter Citations. First, read the introductions on pp. vi-1 and 693 of the Wisconsin volume and pp. v-1 of the Northwestern volume.

15. Find the entry for 52 Wis. 2d 173. What is the parallel citation to the North Western Reporter?
    ANSWER:

16. Additionally, locate the entry for the opinion under its North Western citation in the Wisconsin Shepard's and the Northwestern Shepard's. Looking at the entries for this opinion in all three places, answer the following questions:

    a. Cite the Marquette law review article which refers to 52 Wis. 2d 173. (Write out the name of the law review.)
    ANSWER:

    b. State the citation of the Idaho opinion which cites 52 Wis. 2d 173.
    ANSWER:

    c. What happened in the subsequent history (not treatment) of 52 Wis. 2d 173 after the Wisconsin Supreme Court rendered its decision?
    ANSWER:

17. When Shepardizing a particular citation, where will you find a complete list of the bound volumes and supplements you will need to check?
ANSWER:

ASSIGNMENT XIII
SHEPARD'S CITATORS--CASES
EXERCISE D

GOALS: 1) To give you experience in Shepardizing court opinions, identifying the citing materials, and interpreting their treatment of the cited opinion.

2) To teach you how to use Shepard's to identify parallel citations for either official or unofficial court decisions.

3) To help you internalize the differences in scope of citing materials found in the various sections of Shepard's United States Citations--Cases and found in the Shepard's complementary state and regional reporters.

NOTE: When a case citation appears in your answers, use the standard abbreviation for the reporter as found in A Uniform System of Citation, 13th ed. It may differ substantially from the Shepard's abbreviation. If a law review citation is your answer, write out the title of the law review in full.

To answer Questions 1-4 use only the 1971-1976 Case Edition Supplement of Shepard's United States Citations--Cases (Vol. 4). First read pp. vii-xvii and the introduction to the U.S., L. Ed., and S. Ct. sections on pages 1, 799, and 1273. Note for each section the "citing" materials which have referred to the Supreme Court cases.

1. Using the U.S. section of this volume, state the parallel citations for 400 U.S. 423.
   ANSWER:

2. What is the official Montana Supreme Court citation for this case (i.e., what is the citation to the same case in the immediate court below)?
   ANSWER:

3. In what U.S. Supreme Court decision did the dissent cite 400 U.S. 423? Provide the citation.
   ANSWER:

4. What U.S. District Court opinion explained the decision in 400 U.S. 423? Provide the citation.
   ANSWER:

5. Find the case from Questions 1-4 under its L. Ed. citation in the L. Ed. section. What opinion followed the decision?
   ANSWER:

6. Find the case from Questions 1-5 under its S. Ct. citation in the S. Ct. section. What opinion cited a point of law from West headnote number 1 of the cited case?
   ANSWER:

Now you have examined entries of materials which cite one case in all three sections under each of its citations. Be sure to use the appropriate section when answering Questions 7-11.

7. State the citation of the A.L.R. annotation which cited 29 L. Ed. 2d 810.
   ANSWER:

8. Did the A.L.R. annotation reference to 29 L. Ed. 2d 810 in the previous question appear in the annotation or its supplement? (If you need help with this question, refer back to the last paragraph on p. xi.)
   ANSWER:

9. Find the entry for 79 S. Ct. 451. Why is no parallel citation listed?
   ANSWER:

10. State the citation of the annotation appearing in United States Supreme Court Reports—Lawyers' Edition which referred to 89 S. Ct. 1871.
    ANSWER:

11. What U.S. Circuit Court of Appeals opinion cited Douglas' concurrence with 418 U.S. 298? Provide the citation.
    ANSWER:

12. Which of the three sections lists citing opinions from state courts?

_____ U.S.

_____ L. Ed.

_____ S. Ct.

13. Which of the three sections list citing A.L.R. Fed. annotations?

_____ U.S.

_____ L. Ed.

_____ S. Ct.

14. Which of the three sections lists citing opinions of selected administrative courts?

_____ U.S.

_____ L. Ed.

_____ S. Ct.

To answer Questions 15 and 16, use only the 1970-1981 Supplement to Shepard's California Citations—Cases and the 1977-1980 Supplement to Vol. 2 of Shepard's Pacific Reporter Citations, Parts 1 & 2. First, read the introductions on pp. vii-1 and 753 of the California volume and pp. vii-1 of the Pacific volume.

15. Find the entry for 12 Cal. 3d 204. What is the parallel citation to the Pacific Reporter?
ANSWER:

16. Additionally, locate the entry for the opinion under its <u>Pacific</u> citation in the California Shepard's and the Pacific Shepard's. Looking at the entries for this opinion in all <u>three</u> places, answer the following questions:

    a.   Cite the Virginia law review article which refers to 12 Cal. 3d 204. (Write out the name of the law review.)
        ANSWER:

    b.   State the citation of the Maryland opinion which cites 12 Cal. 3d 204.
        ANSWER:

    c.   What happened in the subsequent <u>history</u> (not treatment) of 12 Cal. 3d 204 after the California Supreme Court rendered its decision?
        ANSWER:

17. When Shepardizing a particular citation, where will you find a complete list of the bound volumes and supplements you will need to check?
    ANSWER:

INTRODUCTION
TO CHAPTER XIV
SHEPARD'S CITATORS
STATUTES AND POPULAR NAMES

The purpose of this assignment is to familiarize you with the process of Shepardizing statutes. Shepardizing a statute will make you aware of the subsequent history of the statute—whether it was later amended, repealed, etc.--and whether any court cases have interpreted the statute, or ruled on its constitutionality. Different abbreviations must be learned when Shepardizing a statute as opposed to an opinion. Also, since codes are republished periodically, you will often find separate entries for the same statutory reference listed in separate sections under different editions of a code. When you are interested in the subsequent history of a particular piece of statutory language which has appeared in several published editions of a code, all of the entries within a Shepard's volume must be checked. Also remember to update your search in the appropriate Shepard's pamphlets.

This exercise will also introduce you to Shepard's Acts and Cases by Popular Name—Federal and State, which is the most complete index to case and statutory popular names. Remember that you can also find references by popular name to code citations and court reports citations in some other places like the two U.S. Supreme Court digests and the United States Code, United States Code Annotated and United States Code Service.

Before beginning this assignment, read the section on "Mechanics of Sheparizing Statutes" in Chapter 9 and read about Shepard's Acts and Cases by Popular Name in the "Other Case-Finding Tools" section of Chapter 5, in Cohen and Berring, How to Find the Law, 8th ed. Also read the pamphlet How to Use Shepard's Citations.

ASSIGNMENT XIV
SHEPARD'S CITATORS
STATUTES AND POPULAR NAMES
EXERCISE B

GOALS: 1) To give you practice at finding out how court or legislative action affected the validity or changed the language of particular statutory sections.

2) To illustrate similarities and differences between statutory Shepardizing and the case citation Shepardizing which was covered in Chapter XIII.

3) To introduce you to the process of Shepardizing other than federal statutory materials, i.e., state code sections, town ordinances, state jury instructions, and court rules.

4) To familiarize you with the principal cross reference guide <u>from</u> popular names of statutes and court decisions <u>to</u> their citations.

NOTE: When a citation appears in your answers, use the standard abbreviation for the reporter, code, or session laws as found in <u>A Uniform System of Citation,</u> 13th ed. It may differ from the Shepard's abbreviation. When a law review citation is the answer, write out the full title of the law review.

To answer Questions 1-4, use <u>only</u> the 1968-1974 Supplement to the 1968 Statute Edition of <u>Shepard's United States Citations—Statutes.</u>

1. Find the Shepard's entry for 26 U.S.C. § 4481(b) (1970).

a. State the citation of the citing opinion which decided whether or not 26 U.S.C. § 4481(b) was constitutional.
ANSWER:

b. How did the court hold?
ANSWER:

2. State the citation for the annotation which cited 26 U.S.C. § 501(b)(13) (1970).
ANSWER:

3. How did Congress affect 26 U.S.C. § 7012(a) (1970)?
ANSWER:

4. Cite the session law which amended 15 U.S.C. § 32 (1970).
ANSWER:

To answer Questions 5-8, use <u>only</u> the 1968-1980 Supplement to <u>Shepard's New Jersey Citations—Cases and Statutes</u>.

5. Did the New Jersey courts hold New Jersey Statutes Annotated (N.J.S.A.) 12 A:9-503 to be constitutional?
   ANSWER:

6. Cite the law review article which discusses N.J.S.A. 17:28-2. (Write out the title of the law review.)
   ANSWER:

7. State the official and unofficial citations for the New Jersey opinion which cited a Hoboken, New Jersey ordinance concerning canvassing by itinerant peddlers.
   ANSWER:

8. State the citation of the federal opinion which cited New Jersey Court Rule 3:6-2.
   ANSWER:

To answer Questions 9 and 10 use <u>only</u> the bound volume of <u>Shepard's Acts and Cases by Popular Name—Federal and State</u>.

9. State the citation for the Beano Act.
   ANSWER:

10. State the citation for the Absent Judge Murder Case.
    ANSWER:

ASSIGNMENT XIV
SHEPARD'S CITATORS
STATUTES AND POPULAR NAMES
EXERCISE C

GOALS: 1) To give you practice at finding out how court or legislative action affected the validity or changed the language of particular statutory sections.
2) To illustrate similarities and differences between statutory Shepardizing and the case citation Shepardizing which was covered in Chapter XIII.
3) To introduce you to the process of Shepardizing other than federal statutory materials, i.e., state code sections, town ordinances, state jury instructions, and court rules.
4) To familiarize you with the principal cross reference guide from popular names of statutes and court decisions to their citations.

NOTE: When a citation appears in your answers, use the standard abbreviation for the reporter, code, or session laws as found in A Uniform System of Citation, 13th ed. It may differ from the Shepard's abbreviation. When a law review citation is the answer, write out the full title of the law review.

To answer Questions 1-4, use only the 1974-1979 Supplement to the 1968 Statute Edition of Shepard's United States Citations—Statutes.

1. Find the Shepard's entry for 18 U.S.C. § 2113(e) (1976).

    a. State the citation of the citing opinion which decided whether or not 18 U.S.C. § 2113(e) was constitutional.
        ANSWER:

    b. How did the court hold?
        ANSWER:

2. State the citation for the annotation which cited 26 U.S.C. § 1014(a) (1976).
    ANSWER:

3. How did Congress affect 28 U.S.C. § 1341 (1976)?
    ANSWER:

4. Cite the session law which amended 26 U.S.C. § 6871(a) (1976).
    ANSWER:

To answer Questions 5-8, use <u>only</u> the 1979 <u>Statute Edition of Shepard's Wisconsin Citations—Constitutions, Statutes,</u> etc.

5. Did the United States District Court hold Wis. Stat. § 811.04 (1977) to be constitutional?
   ANSWER:

6. Cite the law review article which discusses Wis. Stat. § 801.61 (1977). (Write out the title of the law review.)
   ANSWER:

7. State the official and unofficial citations for the Wisconsin opinion which cited a Green Bay, Wisconsin ordinance concerning electric companies.
   ANSWER:

8. State the citation of the law review article which cited Wisconsin Court Rule 18.
   ANSWER:

To answer Questions 9 and 10 use <u>only</u> the bound volume of <u>Shepard's Acts and Cases by Popular Name—Federal and State.</u>

9. State the citation for the Baby Chick Act.
   ANSWER:

10. State the citation for the Boy Scout Case.
    ANSWER:

ASSIGNMENT XIV
SHEPARD'S CITATORS
STATUTES AND POPULAR NAMES
EXERCISE D

GOALS: 1) To give you practice at finding out how court or legislative action affected the validity or changed the language of particular statutory sections.
2) To illustrate similarities and differences between statutory Shepardizing and the case citation Shepardizing which was covered in Chapter XIII.
3) To introduce you to the process of Shepardizing other than federal statutory materials, i.e., state code sections, town ordinances, state jury instructions, and court rules.
4) To familiarize you with the principal cross reference guide from popular names of statutes and court decisions to their citations.

NOTE: When a citation appears in your answers, use the standard abbreviation for the reporter, code, or session laws as found in A Uniform System of Citation, 13th ed. It may differ from the Shepard's abbreviation. When a law review citation is the answer, write out the full title of the law review.

To answer Questions 1-4, use only the 1968 Statute Edition of Shepard's United States Citations—Statutes.

1. Find the Shepard's entry for 26 U.S.C. § 37 (1964).

    a. State the citation of the citing opinion which decided whether or not 26 U.S.C. § 37 was constitutional.
    ANSWER:

    b. How did the court hold?
    ANSWER:

2. State the citation for the annotation which cited 19 U.S.C. § 1593 (1964).
ANSWER:

3. How did Congress affect 18 U.S.C. § 1914 (1964)?
ANSWER:

4. Cite the session law which amended 45 U.S.C. § 351(i) (1964).
ANSWER:

To answer Questions 5-8, use only the 1975-1982 Supplement to the 1970 Statute Edition of Shepard's California Citations—Constitutions, Codes, etc.

5. Did the California Court of Appeal hold Cal. Gov't. Code § 13959 to be constitutional?
   ANSWER:

6. Cite the law review article which discusses Cal. Health & Safety Code § 1376. (Write out the title of the law review.)
   ANSWER:

7. State the official and unofficial citations for the California appellate opinion which cited a Marin County ordinance concerning emergency water supplies during periods of shortage.
   ANSWER:

8. State the citation of the federal opinion which cited California Jury Instructions—Civil (5th ed.) No. 3.77.
   ANSWER:

To answer Questions 9 and 10 use only the bound volume of Shepard's Acts and Cases by Popular Name—Federal and State.

9. State the citation for the Harmful Plant Act.
   ANSWER:

10. State the citation for the Friars Club Case.
    ANSWER:

INTRODUCTION
TO CHAPTER XV
LEGISLATIVE HISTORY—PART 1

The purpose of this exercise is to familiarize you with three of the publications which researchers often use when investigating the legislative history of bills and laws: the Congressional Information Service Annual, the Commerce Clearing House Congressional Index, and the Digest of Public General Bills and Resolutions. There are other helpful publications available. Some of them appear in the next assignment.

Researching legislative histories can be confusing. The publications you will use are complex, and have many more purposes than can be indicated in one or two exercises. Before beginning this exercise, read Chapter 10, "Legislative History", of Cohen and Berring, How to Find the Law, 8th ed.

GOALS: 1)   To give you practice using three basic sources of information concerning the history of a federal law during its congressional bill stage.

2)   To show you that how you find legislative history information differs both in the titles and the indexes you use depending on the piece of information you already know as you begin your research.

3)   To allow you to compare the relative completeness of various kinds of information provided by three basic legislative history research aids so that in future research you will be able to choose the appropriate aid to supply sought after information.

NOTE: When using the Commerce Clearing House Congressional Index (Cong. Index) Subject Index or Status tables, be sure to check to see whether there are really two indexes or tables in the section. CCH updates the Subject Index by means of a Current Subject Index which immediately precedes it. The Bill Status tables are similar. Researchers may not realize that there may be two alphabetical or numerical sequences that they must check.

1.   Assume you are seeking information on the legislative history of P.L. 97-45, which was enacted in 1981. Using the Abstracts volume of the 1981 Congressional Information Service Annual (CIS), find the "Legislative History Citations" section at the back, and in it, the entry for P.L. 97-45.

    a.   What is the name of the act?
    ANSWER:

    b.   What was the date of its enactment?
    ANSWER:

Note that the bill number of the law is H.R. 2120. To answer Questions 2-6, additionally find the entry for P.L. 97-45 in the "Public Laws" section of the 1981 or 1982 (you may use either) Final Digest of Public General Bills and Resolutions (Digest). Also, find the entry for H.R. 2120 in the "Current Status" or "Status of House Bills" sections of volume 2 of the 1981-1982 Cong. Index. You will need to compare and contrast the entries in all three publications.

2.   Looking at the three entries, tell which of the publications lists earlier hearings on the subject matter of House Bill 2120 from Congresses dating back to 1977.
    ANSWER:

3. What is the report number of the House report on House Bill 2120 (summarized in CIS abstract no. H363-18)?
   ANSWER:

4. On what date did the Senate pass House Bill 2120?
   ANSWER:

5. Looking at the three entries, tell which of the publications lists the dates House Bill 2120 was enrolled in the House and Senate.
   ANSWER:

6. Which publication cites the statement the President made regarding the bill?
   ANSWER:

7. Examine the CIS abstract of the committee print from P.L. 97-45's legislative history (summarized in CIS abstract no. H722-4). To do this, use the 1980 Abstracts volume of CIS (but do not reshelve the 1981 Abstracts volume--you will need it later). Using the 1980 Abstracts volume, note the CIS numbers heading each page. Find the abstract of H722-4.

   a. What is the title of the committee print?
      ANSWER:

   b. For which Congressional committee was it prepared?
      ANSWER:

8. Next, examine the CIS abstract of the 1981 Senate hearing on House Bill 2120 (summarized in CIS abstract no. S261-1). Use the 1981 Abstracts volume. Find S261-1.

   a. Which committee held the hearing?
      ANSWER:

   b. On what dates did James H. Mack testify?
      ANSWER:

9. Examine the CIS abstract of the Senate report on a companion bill (summarized in CIS abstract no. S263-28). Use the 1981 Abstracts volume of CIS and find S263-28.

    a.   Which committee published the report?
        ANSWER:

    b.   Did the committee recommend passage of the bill?
        ANSWER:

10. Using both the Index and Abstracts volumes of the 1981 CIS, answer the following questions.

    a.   Find the Index of Subjects and Names in the Index volume. What is the CIS abstract number for the publication indexed in 1981 concerning Darvon?
        ANSWER:

    b.   Identify your answer to Question 10(a) as a type of Congressional publication (hearing, report, document, committee print).
        ANSWER:

    c.   Use the Index of Subjects and Names. On what date did Mary Clark testify about federal paperwork?
        ANSWER:

    d.   Use the Index of Titles. What is the CIS abstract number of a publication titled <u>Libyan Activities</u>?
        ANSWER:

    e.   Use the Index of Bill Numbers. What is the CIS abstract number of a publication relating to House Resolution 287 from the 97th Congress?
        ANSWER:

Assume you are looking for information on Senate Bill 255 from the 97th Congress (1981-1982). Use the 1981-1982 CCH <u>Congressional Index</u> and the 1981 <u>Digest of Public General Bills and Resolutions</u> to answer Questions 11-17. Be sure to check both publications in order to supply the most complete information. (NOTE: in real life, when using the Digests for a particular Congress you might have to use both annual volumes since parts of them do not cumulate. However, for this assignment, use only one year.)

11. Use the "Senate Bills" section in the Cong. Index, and "Other Measures Receiving Action" in the.Digest. Who sponsored Senate Bill 255?
    ANSWER:

12. On what date was Senate Bill 255 introduced?
    ANSWER:

13. Which publication provides a longer summary of Senate Bill 255?
    ANSWER:

14. Did Senate Bill 255 become law?
    ANSWER:

15. Using the appropriate sections, can you find any identical bills or companion bills for Senate Bill 255? If so, list them.
    ANSWER:

Use the Subject Indexes in both publications to answer Question 16. Be sure to use both the "Current Subject Index" and the "Subject Index" in the Cong. Index.

16. Which bills concerned Reyes Syndrome? State which publication lists which bills.
    ANSWER:

17. Were any of the bills from Question 16 enacted into law?
    ANSWER:

ASSIGNMENT XV
LEGISLATIVE HISTORY-PART I
EXERCISE B

GOALS: 1) To give you practice using three basic sources of information concerning the history of a federal law during its congressional bill stage.

2) To show you that how you find legislative history information differs both in the titles and the indexes you use depending on the piece of information you already know as you begin your research.

3) To allow you to compare the relative completeness of various kinds of information provided by three basic legislative history research aids so that in future research you will be able to choose the appropriate aid to supply sought after information.

NOTE: When using the Commerce Clearing House Congressional Index (Cong. Index) Subject Index or Status tables, be sure to check to see whether there are really two indexes or tables in the section. CCH updates the Subject Index by means of a Current Subject Index which immediately precedes it. The Bill Status tables are similar. Researchers may not realize that there may be two alphabetical or numerical sequences that they must check.

1. Assume you are seeking information on the legislative history of P.L. 96-212, which was enacted in 1980. Using the Abstracts volume of the 1980 Congressional Information Service Annual (CIS), find the "Legislative History Citations" section at the back, and in it, the entry for P.L. 96-212.

   a. What is the name of the act?
   ANSWER:

   b. What was the date of its enactment?
   ANSWER:

Note that the bill number of the law is S. 643. To answer Questions 2-6, additionally find the entry for P.L. 96-212 in the "Public Laws" section of the 1980 Final Digest of Public General Bills and Resolutions (Digest). Also, find the entry for S. 643 in the "Current Status" or "Status of Senate Bills" sections of volume 1 of the 1979-1980 Cong. Index. You will need to compare and contrast the entries in all three publications.

2. Looking at the three entries, tell which of the publications lists earlier hearings on the subject matter of Senate Bill 643 from Congresses dating back to 1977.
   ANSWER:

3. What is the report number of the House conference report on Senate Bill 643 (summarized in CIS abstract no. H523-3)?
   ANSWER:

4. On what date did the House pass the conference version of Senate Bill 643?
   ANSWER:

5. Looking at the three entries, tell which of the publications lists the dates Senate Bill 643 was enrolled in the House and Senate.
   ANSWER:

6. Which publication cites the statement the President made regarding the bill?
   ANSWER:

7. Examine the CIS abstract of the older Senate committee print from P.L. 96-212's legislative history (summarized in CIS abstract no. S522-11). To do this, use the 1979 Abstracts volume of CIS (but do not reshelve the 1980 Abstracts volume—you will need it later). Using the 1979 Abstracts volume, note the CIS numbers heading each page. Find the abstract of S522-11.

   a. What is the title of the committee print?
      ANSWER:

   b. For which Congressional committee was it prepared?
      ANSWER:

8. Next, examine the CIS abstract of the 1980 House hearing on Senate Bill 643 (summarized in CIS abstract no. H381-15). Use the 1980 Abstracts volume. Find H381-15.

   a. Which committee held the hearing?
      ANSWER:

   b. On what date did Dick Clark testify?
      ANSWER:

9. Examine the CIS abstract of the 1979 original Senate report on Senate Bill 643 (summarized in CIS abstract no. S523-14). Use the 1979 Abstracts volume of CIS and find S523-14.

    a.   Which committee published the report?
        ANSWER:

    b.   Did the committee recommend passage of the bill?
        ANSWER:

10. Using both the Index and Abstracts volumes of the 1980 CIS, answer the following questions.

    a.   Find the Index of Subjects and Names in the Index volumes. What is the CIS abstract number for the publication indexed in 1980 concerning diethylstilbestrol?
        ANSWER:

    b.   Identify your answer to Question 10(a) as a type of Congressional publication (hearing, report, document, committee print).
        ANSWER:

    c.   Use the Index of Subjects and Names. On what date did Richard J. Grunewald testify about pension plans?
        ANSWER:

    d.   Use the Index of Titles. What is the CIS abstract number of a publication titled Claims Against Vietnam?
        ANSWER:

    e.   Use the Index of Bill Numbers. What is the CIS abstract number of a publication relating to Senate Bill 1507 from the 96th Congress?
        ANSWER:

Assume you are looking for information on Senate Bill 1390 from the 96th Congress (1979-1980). Use the 1979-1980 CCH <u>Congressional Index</u> and the 1980 <u>Digest of Public General Bills and Resolutions</u> to answer Questions 11-17. Be sure to check <u>both</u> publications in order to supply the most complete information. (NOTE: in real life, when using the Digests for a particular Congress you might have to use both annual volumes since parts of them do not cumulate. However, for this assignment, use only one year.)

11. Use the "Senate Bills" section in the Cong. Index, and "Other Measures Receiving Action" in the Digest. Who sponsored Senate Bill 1390?
   ANSWER:

12. On what date was Senate Bill 1390 introduced?
   ANSWER:

13. Which publication provides a longer summary of Senate 1390?
   ANSWER:

14. Did Senate Bill 1390 become law?
   ANSWER:

15. Using the appropriate sections, can you find any identical bills or companion bills for Senate Bill 1390? If so, list them.
   ANSWER:

Use the Subject Indexes in both publications to answer Question 16. Be sure to use both the "Current Subject Index" and the "Subject Index" in the Cong. Index.

16. Which bills concerned copyright? State which publication lists which bills.
   ANSWER:

17. Were any of the bills from Question 16 enacted into law?
   ANSWER:

ASSIGNMENT XV
LEGISLATIVE HISTORY-PART I
EXERCISE C

GOALS: 1) To give you practice using three basic sources of information concerning the history of a federal law during its congressional bill stage.

2) To show you that how you find legislative history information differs both in the titles and the indexes you use depending on the piece of information you already know as you begin your research.

3) To allow you to compare the relative completeness of various kinds of information provided by three basic legislative history research aids so that in future research you will be able to choose the appropriate aid to supply sought after information.

NOTE: When using the Commerce Clearing House Congressional Index (Cong. Index) Subject Index or Status tables, be sure to check to see whether there are really two indexes or tables in the section. CCH updates the Subject Index by means of a Current Subject Index which immediately precedes it. The Bill Status tables are similar. Researchers may not realize that there may be two alphabetical or numerical sequences that they must check.

1. Assume you are seeking information on the legislative history of P.L. 96-8, which was enacted in 1979. Using the Abstracts volume of the 1979 Congressional Information Service Annual (CIS), find the "Legislative History Citations" section at the back, and in it, the entry for P.L. 96-8.

   a. What is the name of the act?
   ANSWER:

   b. What was the date of its enactment?
   ANSWER:

Note that the bill number of the law is H.R. 2479. To answer Questions 2-6, additionally find the entry for P.L. 96-8 in the "Public Laws" section of the 1979 or 1980 (you may use either) Final Digest of Public General Bills and Resolutions (Digest). Also, find the entry for H.R. 2479 in the "Current Status" or "Status of House Bills" sections of volume 2 of the 1979-1980 Cong. Index. You will need to compare and contrast the entries in all three publications.

2. Looking at the three entries, tell which of the publications lists earlier hearings and committee prints on the subject matter of House Bill 2479 from Congresses dating back to 1978.
   ANSWER:

3. What is the report number of the House Conference Report on House Bill 2479 (summarized in CIS abstract no. H383-4)?
   ANSWER:

4. On what date did the Senate pass the conference version of House Bill 2479?
   ANSWER:

5. Looking at the three entries, tell which of the publications lists the dates House Bill 2479 was enrolled in the House and Senate.
   ANSWER:

6. Which publication cites the statement the President made regarding the bill?
   ANSWER:

7. Examine the CIS abstract of the committee print from P.L. 96-8's legislative history (summarized in CIS abstract no. S382-2). To do this, use the 1978 Abstracts volume of CIS (but do not reshelve the 1979 Abstracts volume--you will need it later). Using the 1978 Abstracts volume, note the CIS numbers heading each page. Find the abstract of S382-2.

   a. What is the title of the committee print?
      ANSWER:

   b. For which Congressional committee was it prepared?
      ANSWER:

8. Next, examine the CIS abstract of the 1979 House hearing on House Bill 2479 (summarized in CIS abstract no. H381-17). Use the 1979 Abstracts volume. Find H381-17.

   a. Which committee held the hearing?
      ANSWER:

   b. On what date did Leonard Unger testify?
      ANSWER:

9. Examine the CIS abstract of the original House report on House Bill 2479 (summarized in CIS abstract no. H383-1). Use the 1979 Abstracts volume of CIS and find H383-1.

    a. Which committee published the report?
       ANSWER:

    b. Did the committee recommend passage of the bill?
       ANSWER:

10. Using both the Index and Abstracts volumes of the 1979 CIS, answer the following questions.

    a. Find the Index of Subjects and Names in the Index volume. What is the CIS abstract number for the publication indexed in 1979 concerning primates?
       ANSWER:

    b. Identify your answer to Question 10(a) as a type of Congressional publication (hearing, report, document, committee print).
       ANSWER:

    c. Use the Index of Subjects and Names. On what date did William Dexter testify about taxation of interstate commerce?
       ANSWER:

    d. Use the Index of Titles. What is the CIS abstract number of a publication titled Open Shelf-Life Dating of Food?
       ANSWER:

    e. Use the Index of Bill Numbers. What is the CIS abstract number of a publication relating to House Bill 5138 from the 95th Congress?
       ANSWER:

Assume you are looking for information on House Bill 3927 from the 96th Congress (1979-1980). Use the 1979-1980 CCH <u>Congressional Index</u> and the 1979 <u>Digest of Public General Bills and Resolutions</u> to answer Questions 11-17. Be sure to check both publications in order to supply the most complete information. (NOTE: in real life, when using the Digests for a particular Congress you might have to use both annual volumes since parts of them do not cumulate. However, for this assignment, use only one year.)

11. Use the "House Bills" section in the Cong. Index, and "Other Measures Receiving Action" in the Digest. Who sponsored House Bill 3927?
    ANSWER:

12. On what date was House Bill 3927 introduced?
    ANSWER:

13. Which publication provides a longer summary of House Bill 3927?
    ANSWER:

14. Did House Bill 3927 become law?
    ANSWER:

15. Using the appropriate sections, can you find any identical bills or companion bills for House Bill 3927? If so, list them.
    ANSWER:

Use the Subject Indexes in both publications to answer Question 16. Be sure to use both the "Current Subject Index" and the "Subject Index" in the Cong. Index.

16. Which bills concerned the U.S. flag? State which publication lists which bills.
    ANSWER:

17. Were any of the bills from Question 16 enacted into law?
    ANSWER:

GOALS: 1) To give you practice using three basic sources of information concerning the history of a federal law during its congressional bill stage.

2) To show you that how you find legislative history information differs both in the titles and the indexes you use depending on the piece of information you already know as you begin your research.

3) To allow you to compare the relative completeness of various kinds of information provided by three basic legislative history research aids so that in future research you will be able to choose the appropriate aid to supply sought after information.

NOTE: When using the Commerce Clearing House Congressional Index (Cong. Index) Subject Index or Status tables, be sure to check to see whether there are really two indexes or tables in the section. CCH updates the Subject Index by means of a Current Subject Index which immediately precedes it. The Bill Status tables are similar. Researchers may not realize that there may be two alphabetical or numerical sequences that they must check.

1. Assume you are seeking information on the legislative history of P.L. 95-256, which was enacted in 1978. Using the Abstracts volume of the 1978 Congressional Information Service Annual (CIS), find the "Legislative History Citations" section at the back, and in it, the entry for P.L. 95-256.

a. What is the name of the act?
ANSWER:

b. What was the date of its enactment?
ANSWER:

Note that the bill number of the law is H.R. 5383. To answer Questions 2-6, additionally find the entry for P.L. 95-256 in the "Public Laws" section of the 1978 Final Digest of Public General Bills and Resolutions (Digest). Also, find the entry for H.R. 5383 in the "Current Status" or "Status of House Bills" sections of volume 2 of the 1977-1978 Cong. Index. You will need to compare and contrast the entries in all three publications.

2. Looking at the three entries, tell which of the publications lists earlier hearings and reports on the subject matter of House Bill 5383 from Congresses dating back to 1973.
ANSWER:

3. What is the report number of the 1977 Senate report on House Bill 5383 (summarized in CIS abstract no. S413-30)?
   ANSWER:

4. On what date did the House pass the conference version of House Bill 5383?
   ANSWER:

5. Looking at the three entries, tell which of the publications lists the dates House Bill 5383 was enrolled in the House and Senate.
   ANSWER:

6. Which publication cites the statement the President made regarding the bill?
   ANSWER:

7. Examine the CIS abstract of the House committee print from P.L. 95-256's legislative history (summarized in CIS abstract no. H142-4). To do this, use the 1977 Abstracts volume of CIS (but do not reshelve the 1978 Abstracts volume—you will need it later). Using the 1977 Abstracts volume, note the CIS numbers heading each page. Find the abstract of H142-4.

   a. What is the title of the committee print?
      ANSWER:

   b. For which Congressional committee was it prepared?
      ANSWER:

8. Next, examine the CIS abstract of the 1978 Senate hearing on House Bill 5383 (summarized in CIS abstract no. S411-4). Use the 1978 Abstracts volume. Find S411-4.

   a. Which committee held the hearing?
      ANSWER:

   b. On what date did Marc Rosenblum testify?
      ANSWER:

9. Examine the CIS abstract of the Senate report on House Bill 5383 (summarized in CIS abstract no. S413-30). Use the <u>1977</u> Abstracts volume of CIS and find S413-30.

    a. Which committee published the report?
       ANSWER:

    b. Did the committee recommend passage of the bill?
       ANSWER:

10. Using the 1978 Abstracts volume and the 1975-1978 Index volumes of CIS, answer the following questions.

    a. Find the Index of Subjects and Names in the Index volumes. What is the CIS abstract number for the publication indexed in 1978 concerning suburbs?
       ANSWER:

    b. Identify your answer to Question 10(a) as a type of Congressional publication (hearing, report, document, committee print).
       ANSWER:

    c. Use the Index of Subjects and Names. On what date did Dwane Rennels testify about uranium mill tailings?
       ANSWER:

    d. Use the Index of Titles. What is the CIS abstract number of a publication titled <u>Home Production of Beer and Wine</u>?
       ANSWER:

    e. Use the Index of Bill Numbers. What is the CIS abstract number of a publication relating to House Concurrent Resolution 596 from the 95th Congress?
       ANSWER:

Assume you are looking for information on House Bill 7747 from the 95th Congress (1977-78). Use the 1977-1978 CCH Congressional Index and the 1978 Digest of Public General Bills and Resolutions to answer Questions 11-17. Be sure to check both publications in order to supply the most complete information. (NOTE: in real life, when using the Digests for a particular Congress you might have to use both annual volumes since parts of them do not cumulate. However, for this assignment, use only one year.)

11. Use the "House Bills" section in the Cong. Index, and "Other Measures Receiving Action" in the Digest. Who sponsored House Bill 7747?
    ANSWER:

12. On what date was House Bill 7747 introduced?
    ANSWER:

13. Which publication provides a longer summary of House Bill 7747?
    ANSWER:

14. Did House Bill 7747 become law?
    ANSWER:

15. Using the appropriate sections, can you find any identical bills or companion bills for House Bill 7747? If so, list them.
    ANSWER:

Use the Subject Indexes in both publications to answer Question 16. Be sure to use both the "Current Subject Index" and the "Subject Index" in the Cong. Index.

16. Which bills concerned the confidentiality of medical records? State which publication lists which bills.
    ANSWER:

17. Were any of the bills from Question 16 enacted into law?
    ANSWER:

INTRODUCTION
TO CHAPTER XVI
LEGISLATIVE HISTORY—PART II

This assignment is designed to improve your comparative knowledge of the contents of six sources of legislative history material. The completion of this exercise should go a long way towards equipping you to locate and identify relevant legislative history materials for any piece of federal legislation. If you are unfamiliar with the methods of legislative history research, do not attempt it until you have completed Part I.

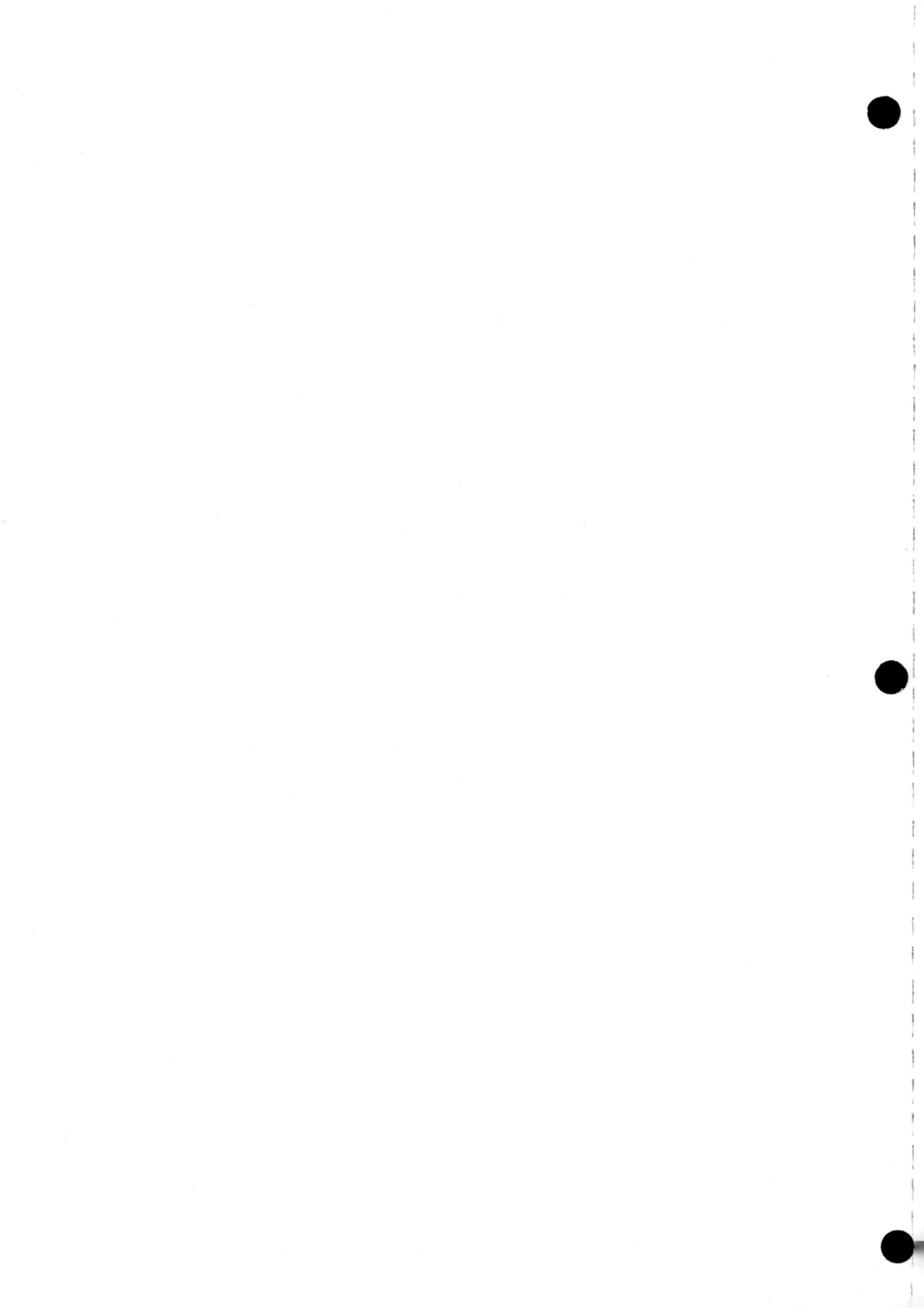

ASSIGNMENT XVI
LEGISLATIVE HISTORY—PART II

GOALS: 1) To build an awareness of which of the six sources of legislative history information can provide specific kinds of documents or specific formats of information.

2) To prepare you to make independent identification of relevant legislative history materials for a federal statute.

In the previous assignment you were introduced to some of the tools for identifying the documents and events of legislative history. Compiling citations and/or texts for a legislative history can be confusing and difficult. To prepare for this assignment, read the publishers' instructions on how to use the following:

Congressional Information Service Index (CIS)

CIS Legislative History Service (LHS). NOTE: Your law library may not have this set, as it is fairly recent. If not, omit LHS as a possible answer.

CCH Congressional Index (Cong. Index)

Digest of Public General Bills and Resolutions (Digest)

United States Code Congressional and Administrative News (U.S. Code Cong. & Ad. News)

Congressional Record (Cong. Rec.)

Also read Chapter 10, "Legislative History," in Cohen and Berring, How to Find the Law, 8th ed.

1. Which of the following publications contain digests (summaries) of bills?

_____ Cong. Index   _____ U.S. Code Cong. & Ad. News

_____ Digest   _____ None of the above

_____ CIS

2. Which of the following publications contain the full texts of all bills?

_____ Cong. Index   _____ LHS

_____ Digest   _____ Cong. Rec.

_____ CIS   _____ None of the above

3. Which of the following trace the course (i.e., cite or refer to hearings, debates, voting) of <u>all public bills</u> through Congress and state whether they become law?

_____	Cong. Index	_____	LHS
_____	Digest	_____	Cong. Rec.
_____	CIS	_____	U.S. Code Cong. & Ad. News

4. Which of the following abstracts (summarizes) and indexes <u>all</u> Congressional reports, documents, hearings, and committee prints?

_____	Cong. Index	_____	LHS
_____	Digest	_____	U.S. Code Cong. & Ad. News
_____	CIS	_____	None of the above

5. Which of the following contains the full texts or lengthy excerpts of selected House and Senate reports?

_____	Cong. Index	_____	LHS
_____	Digest	_____	U.S. Code Cong. & Ad. News
_____	CIS	_____	None of the above

6. Which of the following contains the texts of Congressional debates?

_____	Cong. Index	_____	U.S. Code Cong. & Ad. News
_____	CIS	_____	Cong. Rec.
_____	LHS	_____	None of the above

7. Which publication contains the full texts of new laws?

    _____ Cong. Index   _____ U.S. Code Cong. & Ad.
                                                    News

    _____ Digest   _____ LHS

    _____ CIS   _____ None of the above

8. True or False: the Digest contains abstracts of <u>both bills</u> and <u>laws</u>.
    ANSWER:

9. True or False: the Digest and Cong. Index are fairly similar in what they
    cover.
    ANSWER:

10. True or False: the Digest is usually much more current than the Cong. Index.
    ANSWER:

11. True or False: CIS and LHS are the only two of the six publications which
    will cite Presidential messages (other than vetos) regarding bills.
    ANSWER:

12. True or False: although U.S. Code Cong. & Ad. News does not contain the
    full text of committee prints, it does cite them when they are part of the
    history of a new law.
    ANSWER:

13. True or False: although CIS does not trace the course of all bills introduced
    in Congress, nonetheless its indexes may be used to find Congressional
    publications relating to most bills.
    ANSWER:

14. True or False: whereas CIS provides abstracts of all Congressional reports,
    documents, hearings, and committee prints, LHS provides such abstracts only
    for reports, documents, hearings, and committee prints related to bills that
    have become law.
    ANSWER:

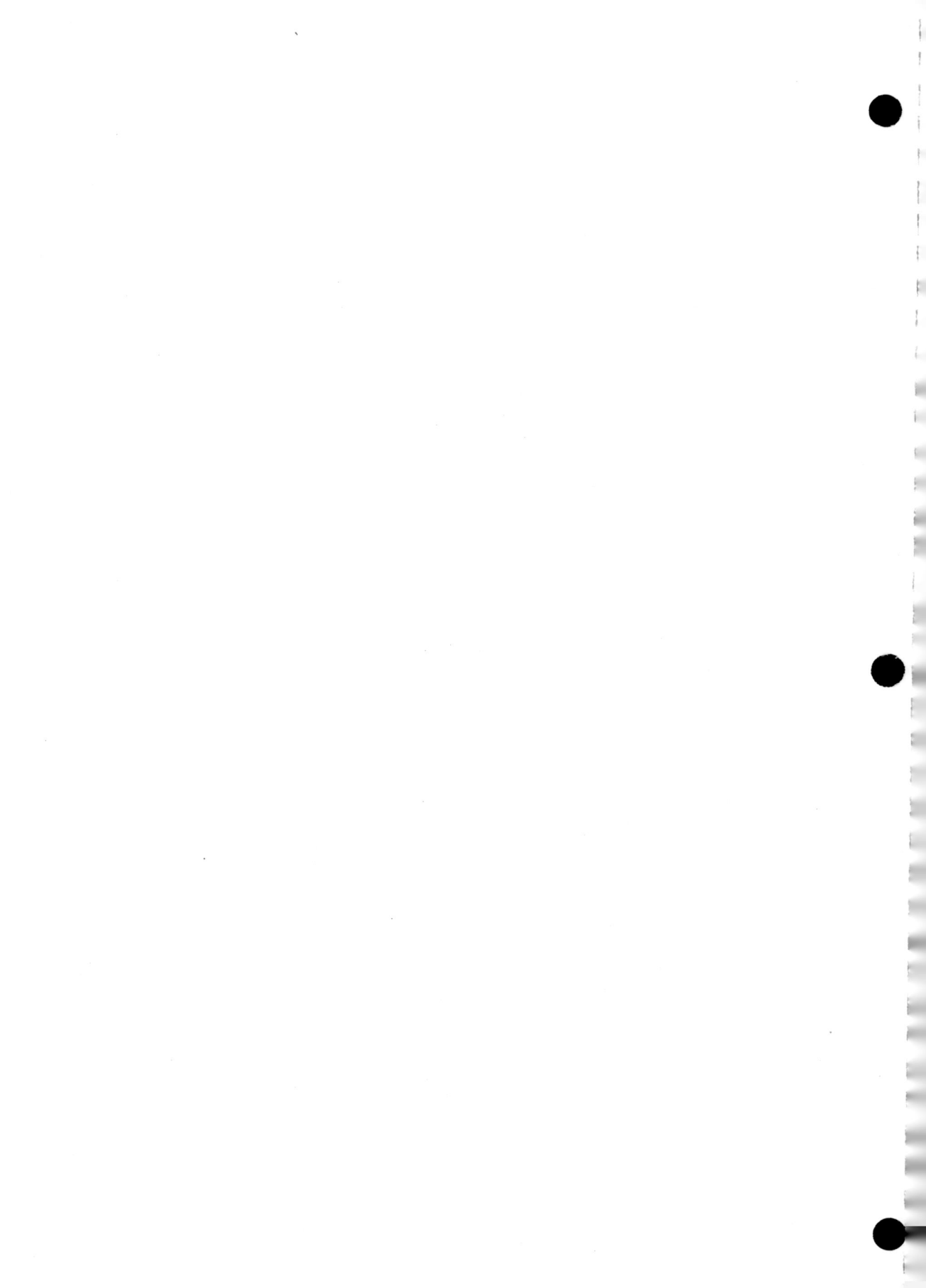

INTRODUCTION
TO CHAPTER XVII
FEDERAL RULES AND REGULATIONS

The purpose of this assignment is to familiarize you with certain aspects of research in federal administrative law. You will have to find a Presidential executive order and a Presidential proclamation. You will have to find and update regulations in the Code of Federal Regulations (C.F.R.). You will use the Federal Register (Fed. Reg.). Many students find the C.F.R. and Federal Register confusing. One way to understand them is to compare them with legislative publications. C.F.R. is analogous to the United States Code. They are both codifications, that is, current, general regulations or laws grouped by subject. The Federal Register is comparable to the United States Statutes at Large (Stat.) They both contain an inclusive, chronological listing of regulations or laws. Of course there are some differences, e.g. the Federal Register contains proposed regulations but Stat. does not contain bills.

To complete this exercise you will need to use any of the publications of your choice which contain Presidential executive orders and proclamations, the Code of Federal Regulations, the C.F.R. List of Sections Affected, the Federal Register, and A Uniform System of Citation, 13th ed.

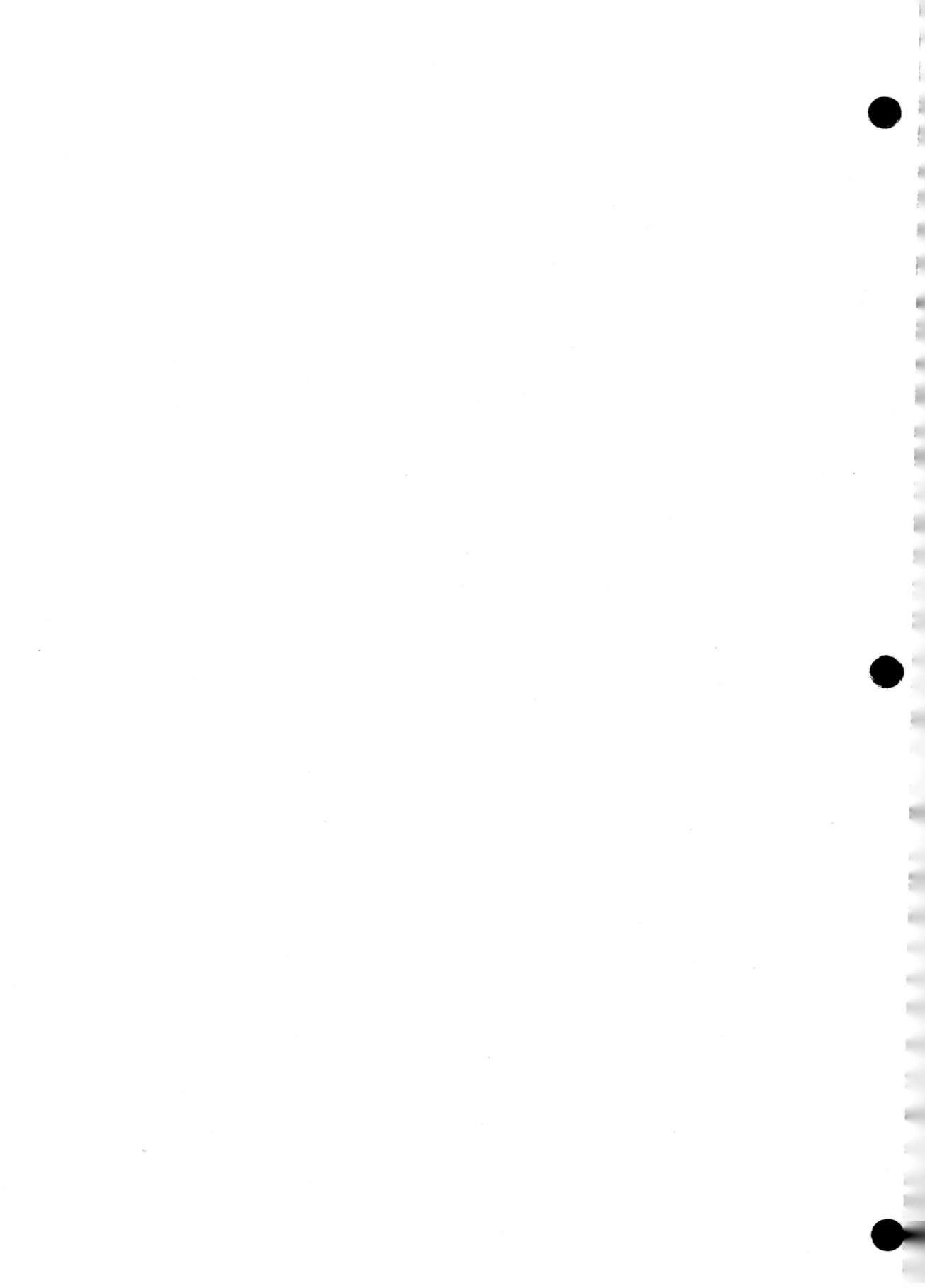

ASSIGNMENT XVII
FEDERAL ADMINISTRATIVE RULES AND REGULATIONS
EXERCISE B

GOALS: 1) To develop your ability to locate printed federal agency regulations on a specific topic, issued by a specific agency, or issued pursuant to authority granted by a particular statute.
2) To give you experience in discovering whether regulatory language has been modified or eliminated since the latest printed C.F.R. version.
3) To give you some facility in locating Presidential documents such as proclamations or executive orders.

PART I: THE PRESIDENT

1. Name three official publications (i.e., published by the U.S. government) in which you can find current executive orders.
ANSWER:

2. Find Executive Order 12323. What is its title?
ANSWER:

3. Presidential proclamations can be found in one official U.S. publication in addition to those you identified in Question 1. What is its title?
ANSWER:

4. What did the President proclaim with Proclamation 4785?
ANSWER:

PART II: AGENCY RULES AND REGULATIONS

To answer Questions 5-9, use the 1981 Code of Federal Regulations.

5. Using the index volume, find the regulations concerning crop insurance for wheat. Provide the complete citation to the subpart dealing with good faith reliance on misrepresentation. Use A Uniform System of Citation, 13th ed., and assume for citation purposes that the regulation is not commonly known by its name.
ANSWER:

6. What is the statutory or executive authority for 7 C.F.R. § 610.3 (1981)?
   State the reference(s) as printed in the C.F.R.
   ANSWER:

7. Where did the regulation in Question 6 originally appear in the <u>Federal
   Register</u>? State the reference(s) as printed in the C.F.R.
   ANSWER:

8. Using the index volume, find Immigration and Naturalization Services
   regulations concerning certificates of citizenship. Provide the complete
   citation to the subpart dealing with examination upon application. Use <u>A
   Uniform System of Citation</u>, 13th ed., and assume for citation purposes that
   the regulation is <u>not</u> commonly known by its name.
   ANSWER:

9. Using the appropriate table in the index volume, state which title and part
   of the C.F.R. was promulgated under the authority of 42 U.S.C. § 299c.
   ANSWER:

The following question is designed to teach you how to discover whether a
regulation published in the C.F.R. has been revised, amended, removed, etc.,
subsequent to its publication. It "walks you through" the procedure for bringing
regulations up to the current date. In order to provide correct answers in the
<u>Instructor's Manual</u>, the exercise has been set at a date in the past.

10. Assume that the date is July 16, 1982, and that you wish to update 30 C.F.R
    § 884 (1981). The 1981 C.F.R. volume was revised (is current) as of July 1,
    1981. The 1982 volume has not yet been published.

    a. Check the June 1982 <u>C.F.R. List of Sections Affected</u> (L.S.A.). This
       pamphlet will update your citation through what date?
       ANSWER:

    b. Has your citation been revised?
       ANSWER:

    c.   On what page of the 1982 Federal Register would you find the revision?
        ANSWER:

    d.   After you have checked the L.S.A., find the Federal Register for July 16, 1982. Find the section in the back titled "C.F.R. Parts Affected during July." Has your citation been affected?
        ANSWER:

To answer Questions 11 and 12, use the 1981 Federal Register.

11.   Using the annual index, locate and cite the following according to A Uniform System of Citation, 13th ed. Assume for citation purposes that each does not have a commonly used name.

    a.   Proposed Farm Credit Administration rules concerning the disposition of obsolete records.
        ANSWER:

    b.   Final Farm Credit Administration rules concerning the disposition of obsolete records.
        ANSWER:

12.   Examine the Federal Register for September 8, 1981.
    a.   Does it contain any proposed rules of the Fish and Wildlife Service?
        ANSWER:

    b.   Does it contain any notices of the Parole Commission?
        ANSWER:

13.   In what publication would you be able to find court cases that cite the Code of Federal Regulations?
    ANSWER:

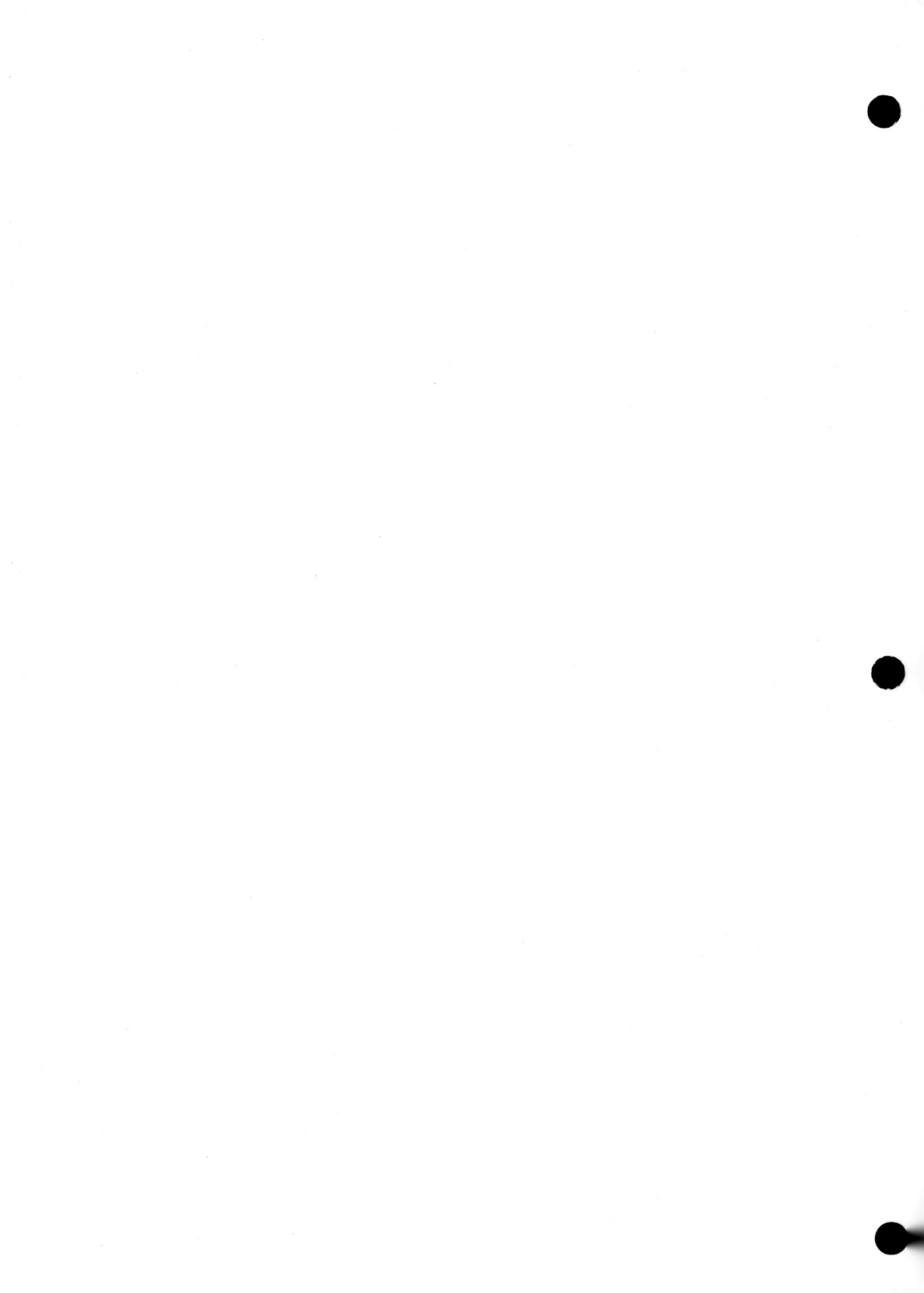

ASSIGNMENT XVII
FEDERAL ADMINISTRATIVE RULES AND REGULATIONS
EXERCISE C

GOALS: 1) To develop your ability to locate printed federal agency regulations on a specific topic, issued by a specific agency, or issued pursuant to authority granted by a particular statute.

2) To give you experience in discovering whether regulatory language has been modified or eliminated since the latest printed C.F.R. version.

3) To give you some facility in locating Presidential documents such as proclamations or executive orders.

PART I: THE PRESIDENT

1. Name three official publications (i.e., published by the U.S. government) in which you can find current executive orders.
    ANSWER:

2. Find Executive Order 12198. What is its title?
    ANSWER:

3. Presidential proclamations can be found in one official U.S. publication in addition to those you identified in Question 1. What is its title?
    ANSWER:

4. What did the President proclaim with Proclamation 4698?
    ANSWER:

PART II: AGENCY RULES AND REGULATIONS

To answer Questions 5-9, use the 1980 Code of Federal Regulations.

5. Using the index volume, find the regulations concerning legal matters of federal prisoners. Provide the complete citation to the subpart dealing with visits by attorneys. Use A Uniform System of Citation, 13th ed., and assume for citation purposes that the regulation is not commonly known by its name.
    ANSWER:

6. What is the statutory or executive authority for 28 C.F.R. § 17.2 (1980)? State the reference(s) as printed in the C.F.R.
ANSWER:

7. Where did the regulation in Question 6 originally appear in the <u>Federal Register</u>? State the reference(s) as printed in the C.F.R.
ANSWER:

8. Using the index volume, find the Commodity Futures Trading Commission's regulations concerning commodity option transactions. Provide the complete citation to the subpart dealing with disclosure. Use <u>A Uniform System of Citation</u>, 13th ed., and assume for citation purposes that the regulation is not commonly known by its name.
ANSWER:

9. Using the appropriate table in the index volume, state which title and part of the C.F.R. was promulgated under the authority of 5 U.S.C. § 171a.
ANSWER:

The following question is designed to teach you how to discover whether a regulation published in the C.F.R. has been revised, amended, removed, etc., subsequent to its publication. It "walks you through" the procedure for bringing regulations up to the current date. In order to provide correct answers in the <u>Instructor's Manual,</u> the exercise has been set at a date in the past.

10. Assume that the date is October 6, 1982, and that you wish to update 49 C.F.R. § 178.51-12 (1981). The 1981 C.F.R. volume was revised (is current) as of October 1, 1981. The 1982 volume has not yet been published.

   a. Check the September, 1982 <u>C.F.R. List of Sections Affected</u> (L.S.A.). This pamphlet will update your citation through what date?
   ANSWER:

   b. Has your citation been revised?
   ANSWER:

c. On what page of the 1981 Federal Register would you find the revision?
ANSWER:

d. After you have checked the L.S.A., find the Federal Register for October 6, 1982. Find the section in the back titled "C.F.R. Parts Affected during October." Has your citation been affected?
ANSWER:

To answer Questions 11 and 12, use the 1982 Federal Register.

11. Using the annual index, locate and cite the following according to A Uniform System of Citation, 13th ed. Assume for citation purposes that each does not have a commonly used name.

a. Proposed rule of the Fair Housing and Equal Opportunity Assistant Secretary concerning the recognition of substantially equivalent state and local fair housing laws.
ANSWER:

b. Final rules of the Fair Housing and Equal Opportunity Assistant Secretary concerning the recognition of substantially equivalent state and local fair housing laws.
ANSWER:

12. Examine the Federal Register for May 24, 1982.
a. Does it contain a proposed rule of the Securities and Exchange Commission?
ANSWER:

b. Does it contain any notices of the Health Care Financing Administration?
ANSWER:

13. In what publication would you be able to find court cases that cite the Code of Federal Regulations?
ANSWER:

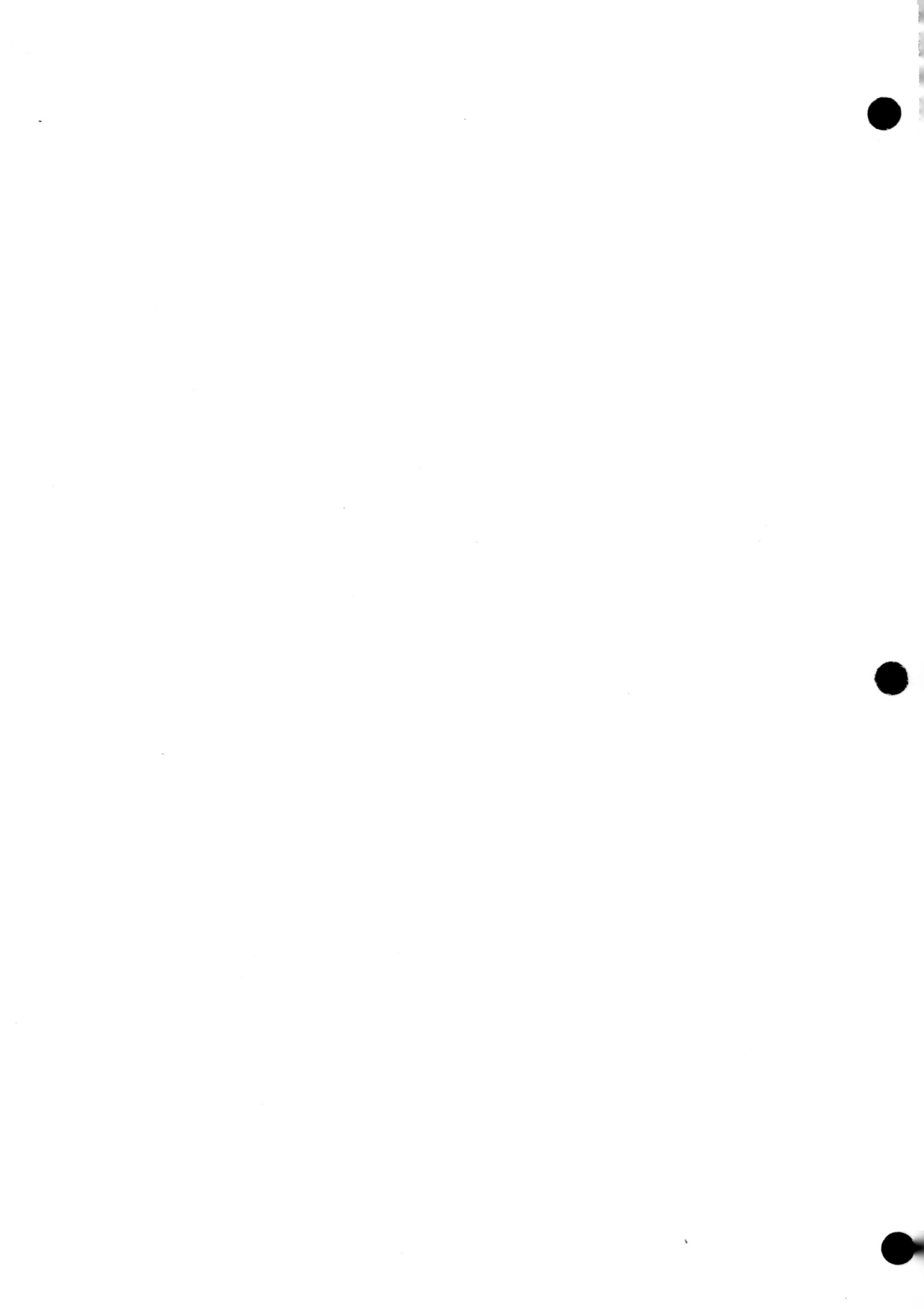

ASSIGNMENT XVII
FEDERAL ADMINISTRATIVE RULES AND REGULATIONS
EXERCISE D

GOALS: 1) To develop your ability to locate printed federal agency regulations on a specific topic, issued by a specific agency, or issued pursuant to authority granted by a particular statute.
2) To give you experience in discovering whether regulatory language has been modified or eliminated since the latest printed C.F.R. version.
3) To give you some facility in locating Presidential documents such as proclamations or executive orders.

PART I: THE PRESIDENT

1. Name three official publications (i.e., published by the U.S. government) in which you can find current executive orders.
ANSWER:

2. Find Executive Order 12123. What is its title?
ANSWER:

3. Presidential proclamations can be found in one official U.S. publication in addition to those you identified in Question 1. What is its title?
ANSWER:

4. What did the President proclaim with Proclamation 4831?
ANSWER:

PART II: AGENCY RULES AND REGULATIONS

To answer Questions 5-9, use the 1982 Code of Federal Regulations.

5. Using the index volume, find the regulations concerning the marketing of Irish potatoes grown in Idaho. Provide the complete citation to the subpart dealing with marketing policy. Use A Uniform System of Citation, 13th ed., and assume for citation purposes that the regulation is not commonly known by its name.
ANSWER:

6. What is the statutory or executive authority for 7 C.F.R. § 904.5 (1982)? State the reference(s) as printed in the C.F.R.
   ANSWER:

7. Where did the regulation in Question 6 originally appear in the Federal Register? State the reference(s) as printed in the C.F.R.
   ANSWER:

8. Using the index volume, find the Energy Department's regulations concerning transportation of plutonium by air. Provide the complete citation to the subpart dealing with national security exemptions. Use A Uniform System of Citation, 13th ed., and assume for citation purposes that the regulation is not commonly known by its name.
   ANSWER:

9. Using the appropriate table in the index volume, state which title and part of the C.F.R. was promulgated under the authority of 47 U.S.C. § 360.
   ANSWER:

The following question is designed to teach you how to discover whether a regulation published in the C.F.R. has been revised, amended, removed, etc., subsequent to its publication. It "walks you through" the procedure for bringing regulations up to the current date. In order to provide correct answers in the Instructor's Manual, the exercise has been set at a date in the past.

10. Assume that the date is January 7, 1982, and that you wish to update 7 C.F.R. § 272.1(g)(16) (1981). The 1981 C.F.R. volume was revised (is current) as of January 1, 1981. The 1982 volume has not yet been published.

    a. Check the December, 1981 C.F.R. List of Sections Affected (L.S.A.). This pamphlet will update your citation through what date?
       ANSWER:

    b. Has your citation been revised?
       ANSWER:

    c.   On what page of the 1981 <u>Federal Register</u> would you find the revision?
       ANSWER:

    d.   After you have checked the L.S.A., find the <u>Federal Register</u> for January 7, 1982. Find the section in the back titled "C.F.R. Parts Affected during January." Has your citation been affected?
       ANSWER:

To answer Questions 11 and 12, use the 1980 <u>Federal Register</u>.

11.   Using the annual index, locate and cite the following according to <u>A Uniform System of Citation</u>, 13th ed. Assume for citation purposes that each does <u>not</u> have a commonly used name.

    a.   Proposed rules of the Heritage Conservation and Recreation Service concerning the establishment of recreation use fees.
       ANSWER:

    b.   Final rules of the Heritage Conservation and Recreation Service concerning the establishment of recreation use fees.
       ANSWER:

12.   Examine the <u>Federal Register</u> for May 7, 1980.
    a.   Does it contain any proposed rules of the Interstate Commerce Commission?
       ANSWER:

    b.   Does it contain any notices of the National Science Foundation?
       ANSWER:

13.   In what publication would you be able to find court cases that cite the <u>Code of Federal Regulations</u>?
    ANSWER:

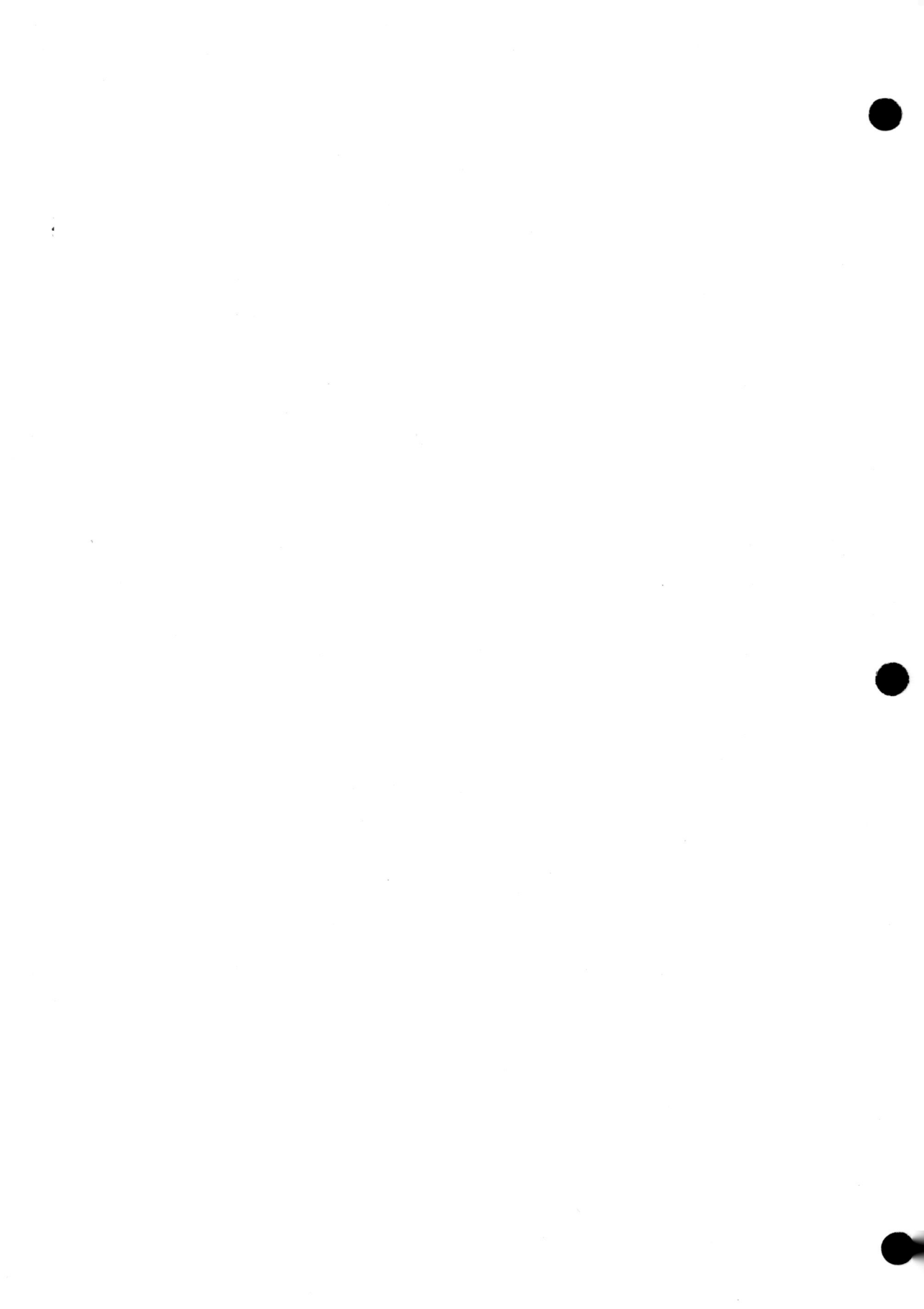

INTRODUCTION
TO CHAPTER XVIII
ADMINISTRATIVE DECISIONS
AND LOOSELEAF SERVICES

Under our system of government, courts are not the only bodies which can settle disputes between parties. Legislatures have delegated this power to selected administrative agencies. The agencies' resolutions of these disputes may be called decisions, orders, or rulings. N.L.R.B. decisions are "decisions" in this sense. One can easily be misled, however, by the equivocal use of technical legal terms; Treasury decisions are not "decisions" at all but are regulations promulgated by the Treasury Dept. During the first part of this assignment you will work with official reports of federal administrative agencies.

During the second part of the assignment you will use a looseleaf service containing, among other materials, the decisions of the administrative agency that you used in the first part of the assignment. Looseleaf services bring together statutes, cases, regulations, and other material (such as commentaries or law review articles) from one subject area. Because of their convenience, they are used extensively by lawyers. We can give you only one tip for looseleaf use, as there is considerable variety among looseleaf services. That tip is, "Read the How to Use section first."

Before beginning this assignment, read "Decisions of the Federal Administrative Agencies" in Chapter 11, "Administrative and Executive Publications," and read all of Chapter 13, "Looseleaf Services," in Cohen and Berring, How to Find the Law, 8th ed.

ASSIGNMENT XVIII
ADMINISTRATIVE DECISIONS
AND LOOSELEAF SERVICES
EXERCISE B

GOALS: 1) To introduce you to the official reports of a federal administrative agency, by requiring you to examine a specific agency decision in the reports.
2) To give you practice in using a looseleaf service, by requiring you to read the instructions for its use, find an agency decision within it, and use some of its indexes.

ADMINISTRATIVE DECISIONS

Find the 1981 decisions of the Occupational Safety and Health Review Commission (O.S.H.A.R.C.) and use them to answer Questions 1-5.

1. Find the party, Kelly Furniture Manufacturing Corp., in the Table of Contents for the December 1981 decisions. List the fiche coordinates of the case involving this party.
ANSWER:

2. Find the decision. Who is the other party?
ANSWER:

3. Is the Commission reviewing this case, or is it decided by an administrative law judge?
ANSWER:

4. Find the order in the case. Were all of the citations affirmed?
ANSWER:

5. Examine the December 1981 microfiche. Do they contain a subject index?
ANSWER:

LOOSELEAF SERVICES

To answer Questions 6 and 7 use BNA's Occupational Safety and Health Reporter.

6. Read the "How to Use" section in the Decisions volume and the "How to File" section in the References volume. Does this looseleaf service contain:

a. Full texts of court decisions?
ANSWER:

b. Full texts of agency decisions or rulings?
ANSWER:

c. If so, name the agencies.
ANSWER:

d. Full texts of relevant federal statutes?
ANSWER:

e. Full texts of relevant federal regulations?
ANSWER:

7. Assume you are seeking the full text of Secretary of Labor v. Vanco Constuction Co., but that you do not know the year of the decision. Start with the looseleaf Table of Cases in the Decisions volume and work backward into the bound volumes of Occupational Safety and Health Cases.

a. State the Occupational Safety and Health Cases citation according to A Uniform System of Citation, 13th ed., pp. 107-114 (omit the case name and date).
ANSWER:

b. Under what numbers is the opinion digested in this service?
ANSWER:

c. Using the Outline of Classifications, tell what subjects the first number from Question 7(b) represents.
ANSWER:

d. Turn to the Index in Volume 1 of the Reference File. In what place in the C.F.R. could you find regulations on eye and face protection during welding?
ANSWER:

ASSIGNMENT XVIII
ADMINISTRATIVE DECISIONS
AND LOOSELEAF SERVICES
EXERCISE C

GOALS: 1) To introduce you to the official reports of a federal administrative agency, by requiring you to examine a specific agency decision in the reports.

2) To give you practice in using a looseleaf service, by requiring you to read the instructions for its use, find an agency decision within it, and use some of its indexes.

ADMINISTRATIVE DECISIONS

Find Volume 46 of the Decisions and Reports of the Securities and Exchange Commission (S.E.C.) and use it to answer Questions 1-5.

1. Find the party, Glenn Woo, in the Table of Decisions and Reports. On what page does the decision involving this party begin?
ANSWER:

2. Find the opinion. What is the full name of the case?
ANSWER:

3. Has an administrative law judge already heard this case at a lower level?
ANSWER:

4. Is the S.E.C.'s order in this case printed here?
ANSWER:

5. Examine this volume. Is there a subject digest or index within it?
ANSWER:

LOOSELEAF SERVICES

To answer Questions 6 and 7 use CCH's Federal Securities Law Reporter.

6. Read the "How to Use this Reporter" section in Volume 1. Does this looseleaf service contain:

a. Full texts of court decisions?
ANSWER:

b. Full texts of agency decisions or rulings?
   ANSWER:

c. If so, name the agencies.
   ANSWER:

d. Full texts of relevant federal statutes?
   ANSWER:

e. Full texts of relevant federal regulations?
   ANSWER:

7. Assume you are seeking Ash v. GAF Corp., but that you do not know the year of the decision. Start with the looseleaf Case Table in the Current volume and work backward into the transfer binders of the Federal Securities Law Reporter.

   a. State the Federal Securities Law Reporter citation according to A Uniform System of Citation, 13th ed., pp. 107-114 (omit the case name and date).
      ANSWER:

   b. To what paragraph numbers in Volume 3 does the opinion refer you?
      ANSWER:

   c. Use the Topical Index in Volume 1. Under what paragraph would you look to find out what required information about bonus plans a proxy statement must contain?
      ANSWER:

   d. Once you have the pertinent paragraph number, in which index can you check for new developments relating to that paragraph? (Reread "How to Use this Reporter" if you can't answer this question.)
      ANSWER:

ASSIGNMENT XVIII
ADMINISTRATIVE DECISIONS
AND LOOSELEAF SERVICES
EXERCISE D

GOALS: 1) To introduce you to the official reports of a federal administrative agency, by requiring you to examine a specific agency decision in the reports.

2) To give you practice in using a looseleaf service, by requiring you to read the instructions for its use, find an agency decision within it, and use some of its indexes.

ADMINISTRATIVE DECISIONS

Find Volume 1982-1 of the Internal Revenue Cumulative Bulletin and use it to answer Questions 1-5.

1. Find Revenue Ruling 82-98 in the Numerical Finding List. On what page does the opinion begin?
   ANSWER:

2. Find the ruling. What section of the Internal Revenue Code is mentioned in the issue?
   ANSWER:

3. Has an administrative law judge already heard this case at a lower level?
   ANSWER:

4. Find the Holding. Is any part of the amount paid for medical bills subject to the gift tax?
   ANSWER:

5. Examine this volume. Is there a subject digest or index within it?
   ANSWER:

LOOSELEAF SERVICES

To answer Questions 6 and 7 use Prentice-Hall's 1983 Federal Taxes.

6. Read the "How to Use this Service" section in Volume 1. Does this looseleaf service contain:

   a. Full texts of court decisions?
      ANSWER:

233

b. Full texts of agency decisions or rulings?
    ANSWER:

c. If so, name the agencies.
    ANSWER:

d. Full texts of relevant federal statutes?
    ANSWER:

e. Full texts of relevant federal regulations?
    ANSWER:

7. Assume you are seeking the full text of Revenue Ruling 83-13 in this
    service. Start with the "How to Use this Service" section.

    a. Find it and cite it according to A Uniform System of Citation, 13th
        ed., p. 78 (use the I.R.B. form of citation).
        ANSWER:

    b. Read the introductory material for the ruling carefully. You are
        referred to two different subject areas under which this ruling is
        digested: investment credit and depreciation. The paragraph number
        of depreciation is ¶15,002. What is the paragraph number of investment
        credit?
        ANSWER:

    c. Find the paragraph number from the preceding question in Vol. 2 of
        1983 Federal Taxes. What is the name of the Tax Court decision
        concerning a farm building to which you are referred?
        ANSWER:

    d. Turn to the beginning of this paragraph, and read the "P-H Explanation."
        Will grain storage bins qualify for the investment credit?
        ANSWER:

INTRODUCTION
TO CHAPTER XIX
ENCYCLOPEDIAS

The following exercise will acquaint you with <u>Corpus Juris Secundum</u> and <u>American Jurisprudence 2d</u>, the two general legal encyclopedias. Each set has not only a general index at the end, like nonlegal encyclopedias you have used, but also topic or title indexes at the ends of each volume (if a topic fills several volumes, only the last will contain a title index.) When answering questions in this assignment, remember to check the pocket parts. You will also be using the Am. Jur. 2d <u>Desk Book</u>. Most libraries shelve this with Am. Jur. 2d.

Before beginning the assignment, read the section on <u>Corpus Juris Secundum</u> in West's <u>Law Finder</u>, the section on <u>American Jurisprudence 2d</u> in <u>The Living Law</u>, and Chapter 14 of Cohen and Berring, <u>How to Find the Law</u>, 8th ed.

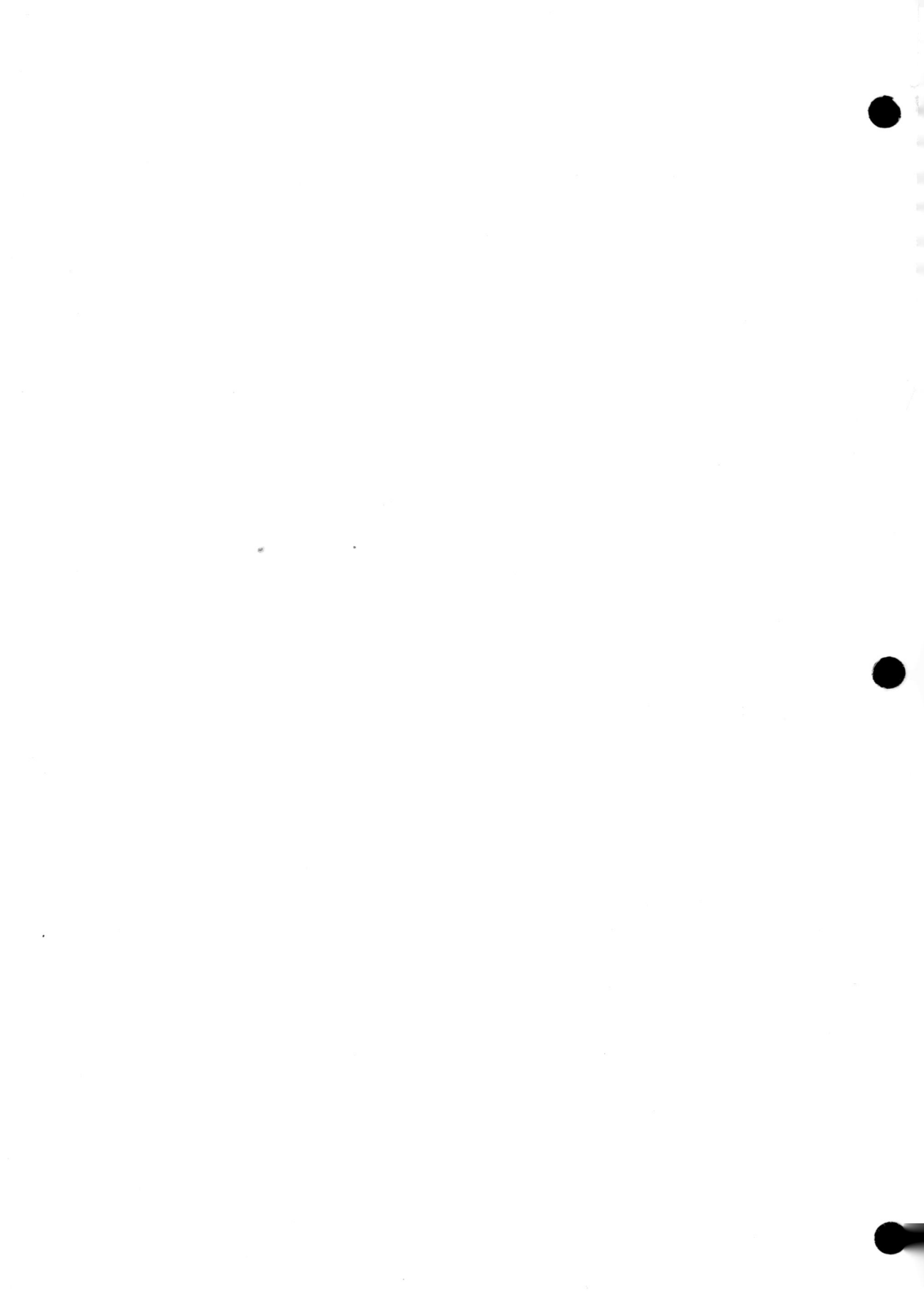

ASSIGNMENT XIX
ENCYCLOPEDIAS
EXERCISE B

GOALS: 1) To familiarize you with the use of the two major legal encyclopedias.
2) To acquaint you with their similarities and differences.

Answer Questions 1-6 using Corpus Juris Secundum.

1. In what volume(s) of Corpus Juris Secundum do you find the general topic Criminal Law?
   ANSWER:

2. Examine the title index for Criminal Law. State the number of the section which discusses the judge's presence at the trial.
   ANSWER:

3. Look up the section. According to the "black letter rule," in the absence of the defendant's waiver or the suspension of proceedings, may a judge be absent from a felony trial?
   ANSWER:

4. State the name of a federal opinion holding that the judge's absence during the selection of a jury was not improper.
   ANSWER:

5. Does this section refer you to a related West topic and key number? If so, state them.
   ANSWER:

6. Using the appropriate volume of C.J.S., state the definition of "crimp."
   ANSWER:

Answer Questions 7-9 using <u>American Jurisprudence 2d.</u>

7. State the volume, title (topic), and section number of the Am. Jur. 2d
    sections which discuss champerty used as a defense.
    ANSWER:

8. State the name of the recent Florida decision which is pertinent to these
    sections.
    ANSWER:

9. Using the appropriate volume, state the Am. Jur. 2d title (topic) and section
    which cites the Model Business Corporation Act § 1.
    ANSWER:

10. Use the Am. Jur. 2d <u>Desk Book.</u> What is the name of the Maine court of
    last resort?
    ANSWER:

ASSIGNMENT XIX
ENCYCLOPEDIAS
EXERCISE C

GOALS: 1) To familiarize you with the use of the two major legal encyclopedias.
2) To acquaint you with their similarities and differences.

Answer Questions 1-6 using Corpus Juris Secundum.

1. In what volume(s) of Corpus Juris Secundum do you find the general topic Evidence?
    ANSWER:

2. Examine the title index for Evidence. State the number of the section which discusses judicial notice of the phenomena of plant life.
    ANSWER:

3. Look up the section. According to the "black letter rule," may courts take judicial notice of facts of common knowledge relating to plant life?
    ANSWER:

4. State the name of a Mississippi opinion where judicial notice was taken of the tendency of wood to rot or decay.
    ANSWER:

5. Does this section refer you to a related West topic and key number? If so, state them.
    ANSWER:

6. Using the appropriate volume of C.J.S., state the definition of "exceptio probat regulam."
    ANSWER:

Answer Questions 7-9 using <u>American Jurisprudence 2d</u>.

7. State the volume, title (topic), and section number of the Am. Jur. 2d section which discusses pretrial statements made in a divorce proceeding.
    ANSWER:

8. State the name of the 1981 New York decision which is pertinent to this section.
    ANSWER:

9. Using the appropriate volume, state the Am. Jur. 2d title (topic) and section which cites the Uniform Marriage and Divorce Act § 407.
    ANSWER:

10. Use the Am. Jur. 2d <u>Desk Book</u>. What is the meaning of "ad damnum"?
    ANSWER:

GOALS: 1) To familiarize you with the use of the two major legal encyclopedias.
2) To acquaint you with their similarities and differences.

Answer Questions 1-6 using Corpus Juris Secundum.

1. In what volume(s) of Corpus Juris Secundum do you find the general topic Fraud?
    ANSWER:

2. Examine the title index for Fraud. State the number of the section which discusses the accrual of a right of action.
    ANSWER:

3. Look up the section. According to the "black letter rule," upon the successful consummation of the fraud when does a cause of action in fraud begin?
    ANSWER:

4. State the name of an Oklahoma opinion where plaintiff's action was held premature.
    ANSWER:

5. Does this section refer you to a related West topic and key number? If so, state them.
    ANSWER:

6. Using the appropriate volume of C.J.S., state the definition of "garba."
    ANSWER:

Answer Questions 7-9 using <u>American Jurisprudence 2d</u>.

7.   State the volume, title (topic) and section number of the Am. Jur. 2d section which discusses commission of a felony as grounds for escheat.
     ANSWER:

8.   State the name of a recent Pennsylvania decision which is pertinent to this section.
     ANSWER:

9.   Using the appropriate volume, state the Am. Jur. 2d title (topic) and section which cites Rule 6 of the Rules of the U.S. Court of Claims.
     ANSWER:

10. Use the Am. Jur. 2d <u>Desk Book</u>. If you saw the abbreviation AHF on a medical record, what would it stand for?
     ANSWER:

INTRODUCTION
TO CHAPTER XX
RESTATEMENTS, FORMBOOKS AND UNIFORM LAWS

    This assignment will introduce you to the three categories of legal materials. While you will not use Restatements and uniform laws every day as an attorney, nevertheless, the legal volumes containing them are important. Formbooks have a more immediate importance, as attorneys use a myriad of forms regularly and also draft their own.

    Before beginning this assignment, read about Restatements and formbooks in Chapter 15 of Cohen and Berring, How to Find the Law, 8th ed. Also read about uniform laws in Chapter 7.

ASSIGNMENT XX
RESTATEMENTS, FORMBOOKS AND UNIFORM LAWS
EXERCISE B

GOALS: 1) To introduce you to a particular Restatement of the Law and give you practice at using it.
2) To show you how to find cases and law review articles which cite Restatements.
3) To introduce you to formbooks.
4) To acquaint you with uniform laws and give you practice at finding them.

RESTATEMENTS

1. Using the Index to the Restatement of Judgments 2d (at the end of Vol. 2, §§ 43 to End), find the Restatement section which concerns actions by bailees or bailors.

a. Cite the section according to A Uniform System of Citation, 13th ed.
ANSWER:

b. According to this section, consider the following: X stores goods in Y's warehouse. If Z burns down the warehouse, may X and Y each sue Z for the full value of the goods?
ANSWER:

2. Use the Appendix of the Restatement of Judgments 2d to answer the following questions.

a. State the name of the 1971 9th Circuit decision that cited § 69 of the First Restatement of Judgments.
ANSWER:

b. To what West topic and key numbers would § 13 of the Restatement of Judgments 2d most closely correspond?
ANSWER:

c. State the name of the 1980 Oregon Court of Appeals decision that cited § 25 of the Restatement of Judgments 2d.
ANSWER:

3. Use the 1976 bound volume of Shepard's Restatement of the Law Citations. State the citation of the law review article which cited § 89, comment j, of the First Restatement of Judgments.
    ANSWER:

FORMBOOKS

Questions 4-6 will require you to find legal forms. Use only the formbook named in the question. Answer by stating the volume and page number where you found the form.

4. Use Rabkin and Johnson, Current Legal Forms with Tax Analysis. Where can you find the form for a provision in a will leaving property to an alien?
    ANSWER:

5. Use Am. Jur. Legal Forms 2d. Where can you find a form for an antenuptial agreement that mentions consideration?
    ANSWER:

6. Use Federal Procedural Forms, L. Ed. Where can you find a form for an application to modify an arbitration award?
    ANSWER:

UNIFORM LAWS

To answer Questions 7-10, use Uniform Laws Annotated.

7. Is the Uniform Child Custody Jurisdiction Act currently in force in Texas?
    ANSWER:

8. Find § 3 of the Uniform Alcoholism and Intoxication Treatment Act. What changes did Colorado make in this section when it adopted the act?
ANSWER:

9. Using the Directory, Tables and Index pamphlet, list the uniform law or laws that concern community property.
ANSWER:

10. State the name of the 1980 New York decision which discusses § 2-720 of the Uniform Commercial Code.
ANSWER:

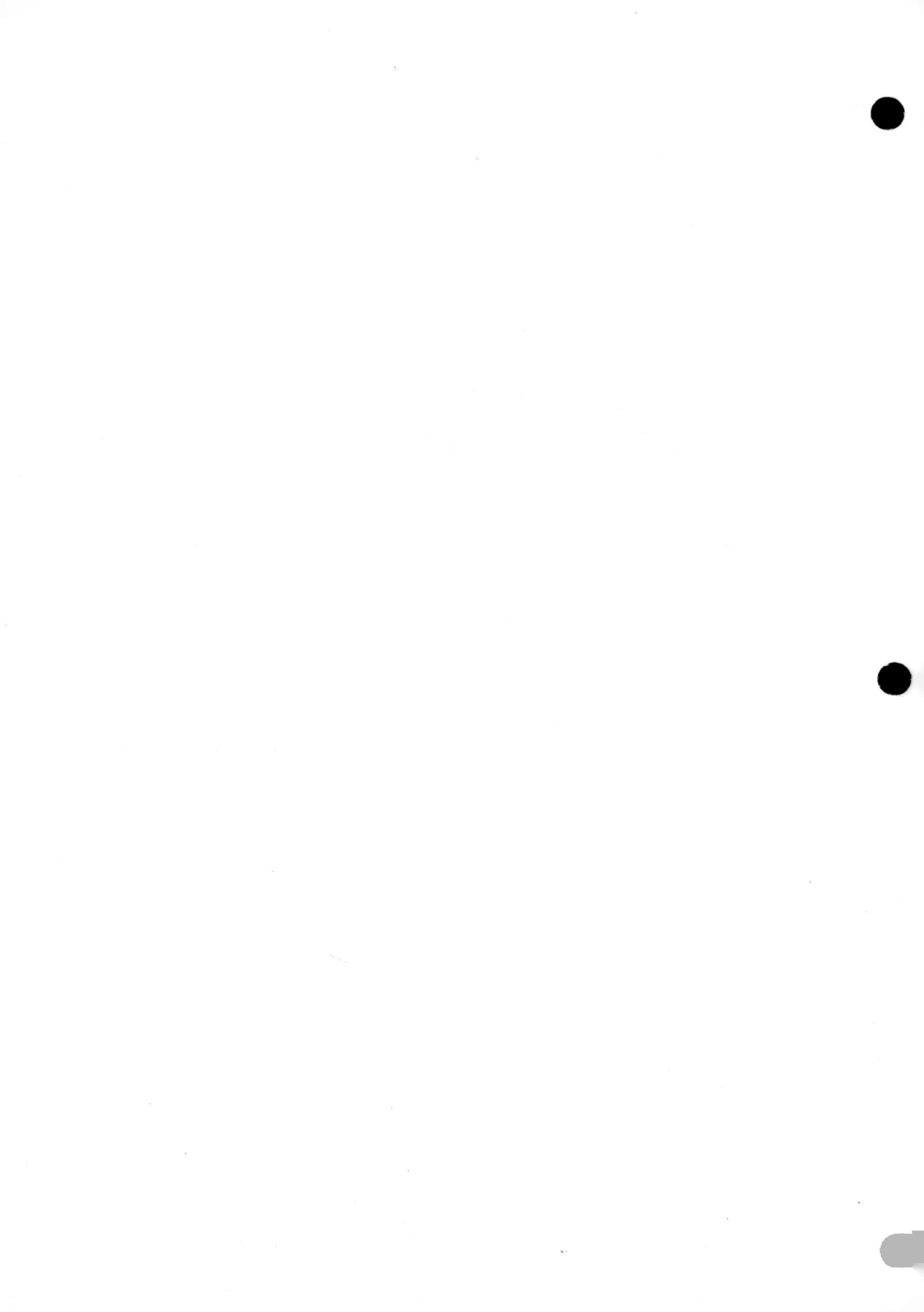

ASSIGNMENT XX
RESTATEMENTS, FORMBOOKS AND UNIFORM LAWS
EXERCISE C

GOALS: 1) To introduce you to a particular Restatement of the Law and give you practice at using it.
2) To show you how to find cases and law review articles which cite Restatements.
3) To introduce you to formbooks.
4) To acquaint you with uniform laws and give you practice at finding them.

RESTATEMENTS

1. Using the Index to the Restatement of Contracts 2d (at the end of Vol. 3, §§ 316 to End), find the Restatement section which discusses the one-year provision of the Statute of Frauds.

    a. Cite the section according to A Uniform System of Citation, 13th ed.
    ANSWER:

    b. According to this section, consider the following: X sells and delivers wheat to Y. If Y orally promises to pay $500 in six months, $500 in twelve months, and $500 in eighteen months, is X forbidden from enforcing the agreement by the Statute of Frauds?
    ANSWER:

2. Use the Appendix volume of the Restatement of Contracts 2d which covers the Restatement 2d to answer the following questions.

    a. State the name of the 1951 California Supreme Court decision that cited § 503 of the First Restatement of Contracts.
    ANSWER:

    b. To what West topic and key numbers would § 283 of the Restatement of Contracts 2d most closely correspond?
    ANSWER:

    c. State the name of the 1978 New York Supreme Court decision that cited § 90 of the Restatement of Contracts 2d.
    ANSWER:

3. Use the 1976 bound volume of Shepard's Restatement of the Law Citations. State the citation of the law review article which cited § 474, comment d, of the First Restatement of Contracts.
   ANSWER:

FORMBOOKS

Questions 4-6 will require you to find legal forms. Use only the formbook named in the question. Answer by stating the volume and page number where you found the form.

4. Use Am. Jur. Legal Forms 2d. Where can you find a form for a living will?
   ANSWER:

5. Use Rabkin and Johnson, Current Legal Forms with Tax Analysis. Where can you find a form for a notice of a corporate directors' meeting?
   ANSWER:

6. Use West's Federal Forms. Where can you find an example of the table of contents of the petitioner's brief on the merits for the U.S. Supreme Court?
   ANSWER:

UNIFORM LAWS

To answer Questions 7-10, use Uniform Laws Annotated.

7. Is the Uniform Anatomical Gift Act currently in force in Nevada?
   ANSWER:

8. Find § 3 of the Uniform Disposition of Unclaimed Property Act. What changes did Iowa make in this section when it adopted the act?
   ANSWER:

9. Using the Directory, Tables and Index pamphlet, list the uniform law or laws that concern assumption of risk.
   ANSWER:

10. State the name of the 1980 Oklahoma decision which discusses § 9-106 of the Uniform Commercial Code.
    ANSWER:

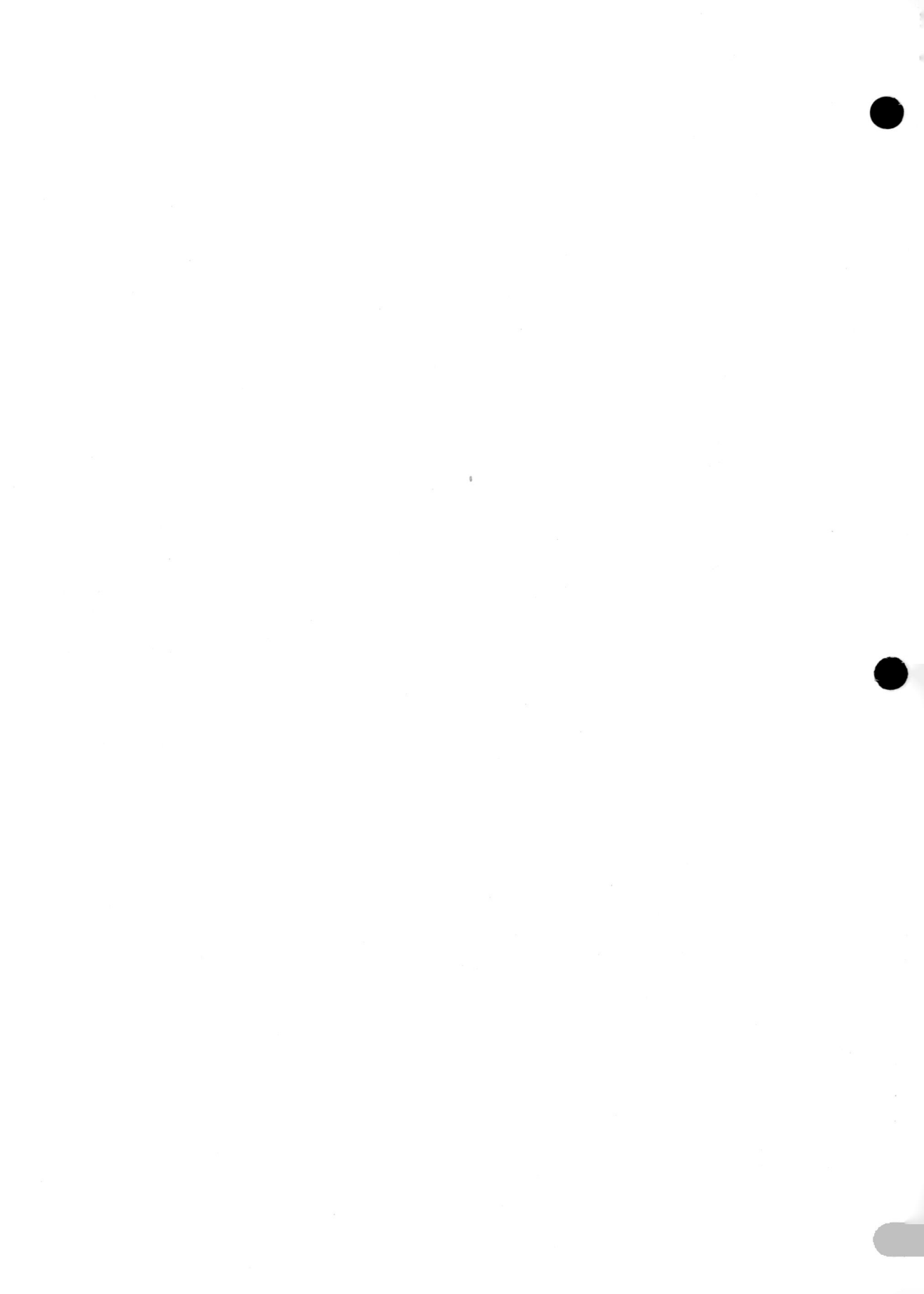

ASSIGNMENT XX
RESTATEMENTS, FORMBOOKS AND UNIFORM LAWS
EXERCISE D

GOALS: 1) To introduce you to a particular Restatement of the Law and give you practice at using it.
2) To show you how to find cases and law review articles which cite Restatements.
3) To introduce you to formbooks.
4) To acquaint you with uniform laws and give you practice at finding them.

RESTATEMENTS

1. Using the Index to the Restatement of Agency 2d (at the end of Vol. 2, §§ 284 to End), find the Restatement section which concerns the standard of care that an agent owes his or her principal.

   a. Cite the section according to A Uniform System of Citation, 13th ed.
   ANSWER:

   b. According to this section, consider the following: X, who repairs computers, hires Y, who represents that he is an expert computer repairman, and Y severely damages a computer which X is trying to repair. If X knows that Y's representation was false, may X sue Y for the damage?
   ANSWER:

2. Use the Appendix of the Restatement of Agency 2d to answer the following questions.

   a. State the name of the 1945 Nebraska decision that cited § 409 of the First Restatement of Agency.
   ANSWER:

   b. To what West topic and key numbers would § 412 of the Restatement of Agency 2d most closely correspond?
   ANSWER:

   c. State the name of the 1978 Maryland decision that cited § 213 of the Restatement of Agency 2d.
   ANSWER:

3. Use the 1976 bound volume of <u>Shepard's Restatement of the Law Citations.</u>
State the citation of the law review article which cited § 151 of the
<u>Restatement of Agency 2d</u>.
ANSWER:

FORMBOOKS

Questions 4-6 will require you to find legal forms. Use only the formbook named
in the question. Answer by stating the volume and page number where you
found the form.

4. Use <u>Am. Jur. Legal Forms 2d</u>. Where can you find a form for the adoption
of an adult?
ANSWER:

5. Use <u>West's Legal Forms</u>, 2d ed. Where can you find a form for a stock
option-warrant?
ANSWER:

6. Use <u>Am. Jur. Pleading and Practice Forms (Revised)</u>. Where can you find
a form for instructions to a jury that an oral agreement falling within the
Statute of Frauds is a bar to action?
ANSWER:

UNIFORM LAWS

To answer Questions 7-10, use <u>Uniform Laws Annotated.</u>

7. Is the Uniform Perpetuation of Testimony Act currently in force in
Oklahoma?
ANSWER:

8. Find § 9 of the Uniform Voting by New Residents in Presidential Elections Act. What changes did North Dakota make in this section when it adopted the act?
   ANSWER:

9. Using the Directory, Tables and Index pamphlet, list the uniform law or laws that concern forgery.
   ANSWER:

10. State the name of the 1977 Michigan Court of Appeals decision which discusses § 6-111 of the Uniform Commercial Code.
    ANSWER:

This assignment will require you to use the two major legal periodical indexes and to cite articles according to A Uniform System of Citation, 13th ed. Since some of the explanations of the indexes' features are misleading, we have drawn up the chart on the next page to help you see at a glance what you can and cannot find in each index, together with the name of the location containing the information.

To complete this assignment you will use A Uniform System of Citation (13th ed.), Index to Legal Periodicals, Current Law Index, various volumes of law reviews, and Shepard's Law Review Citations. Before beginning this assignment, read Chapter 16, "Periodical Literature," in Cohen and Berring, How to Find the Law, 8th ed.

FEATURE	INDEXED IN INDEX TO LEGAL PERIODICALS		INDEXED IN CURRENT LAW INDEX	
Author of Article	Yes	Subject and Author	Yes	Author/Title
Title of Article	No		No	
Subject of Article	Yes	Subject and Author	Yes	Subject
Author of Reviewed Book	Yes	Book Review	Yes	Author/Title
Title of Reviewed Book	Yes if no author	Book Review	Yes	Author/Title
Author of Book Review	No		No	
Title of Book Review	No		No	
Statute	Yes since 1980	Table of Statutes	Yes	Table of Statutes
Cases	*Yes	Table of Cases	**Yes	Table of Cases

*Only current cases commented on in a substantive manner are included. Indexed by plaintiff only.
**Contains all cases given substantial analysis in indexed articles. Indexed by plaintiff and defendant.

ASSIGNMENT XXI
LEGAL PERIODICAL INDEXES
EXERCISE B

GOALS: 1) To introduce you to the two leading legal periodical indexes.
2) To make you familiar with the differences in indexing formats, so that you will be able to use them effectively and without misinterpretation.
3) To give you practice at citing law review articles, comments, casenotes, and book reviews according to A Uniform System of Citation, 13th ed.
4) To show you how to find law review articles and cases which have cited a particular law review article.

NOTE: When you are asked to provide a complete citation, state all information according to A Uniform System of Citation, 13th ed., Rule 16, in the typeface style for briefs and memoranda. It will be necessary to examine the article itself before citing it, because there are often differences between the title of the article and the title listed in the index, and in order to tell whether a student has written the material.

To answer Questions 1-4, use Cumulation 16 of the Index to Legal Periodicals. Each question can be answered from an entry or entries in that volume.

1. Using the Subject and Author Index, provide the complete citation to an article on declaratory relief published in the Vanderbilt Law Review.
   ANSWER:

2. Using the Subject and Author Index, list the titles of the articles written by Abraham L. Gitlow.
   ANSWER:

3. Using the Table of Cases, state how many articles, casenotes, or comments were written about Plasterers Local 79 v. N.L.R.B.
   ANSWER:

4. Using the Book Review Index, provide the complete citation for the review of a book by Hannah Arendt, On Violence.
   ANSWER:

To answer Questions 5-11, use Volume 2 of the Current Law Index. Each question can be answered from an entry or entries in that volume.

5. Using the Author/Title Index, list the titles of the articles written by David T. Austern.
   ANSWER:

6. Using the Table of Cases, tell how many articles, casenotes, or comments discussed a case in which the defendant's name was Roper.
   ANSWER:

7. State the name of the case from Question 6.
   ANSWER:

8. Using the Author/Title Index, provide the complete citation for a book review of See No Evil.
   ANSWER:

9. What grade did the Current Law Index assign the book in the review from Question 8?
   ANSWER:

10. Use the Table of Statutes. In what law review did an article, casenote, or comment discussing the Uniform Comparative Fault Act appear? Abbreviate the title according to A Uniform System of Citation, 13th ed.
ANSWER:

11. Using the Subject Index, provide the complete citation to an article on limited liability which was published in the University of Toledo Law Review.
ANSWER:

12. Using only the 1979 bound volume of Shepard's Law Review Citations, state how many law review articles cited 36 University of Detroit Journal of Urban Law 636.
ANSWER:

ASSIGNMENT XXI
LEGAL PERIODICAL INDEXES
EXERCISE C

GOALS: 1) To introduce you to the two leading legal periodical indexes.
2) To make you familiar with the differences in indexing formats, so that you will be able to use them effectively and without misinterpretation.
3) To give you practice at citing law review articles, comments, casenotes, and book reviews according to A Uniform System of Citation, 13th ed.
4) To show you how to find law review articles and cases which have cited a particular law review article.

NOTE: When you are asked to provide a complete citation, state all information according to A Uniform System of Citation, 13th ed., Rule 16, in the typeface style for briefs and memoranda. It will be necessary to examine the article itself before citing it, because there are often differences between the title of the article and the title listed in the index, and in order to tell whether a student has written the material.

To answer Questions 1-4, use Cumulation 17 of the Index to Legal Periodicals. Each question can be answered from an entry or entries in that volume.

1. Using the Subject and Author Index, provide the complete citation to an article on citizenship published in the Arizona Law Review.
   ANSWER:

2. Using the Subject and Author Index, list the titles of the articles written by David R. Brink.
   ANSWER:

3. Using the Table of Cases, state how many articles, casenotes, or comments were written about Erznoznik v. Jacksonville.
   ANSWER:

4. Using the Book Review Index, provide the complete citation for the review of a book by Henry Cecil, Brief to Counsel.
   ANSWER:

To answer Questions 5-11, use Volume 1 of the Current Law Index. Each question can be answered from an entry or entries in that volume.

5. Using the Author/Title Index, list the titles of the articles written by Christine M. Chinkin.
   ANSWER:

6. Using the Table of Cases, tell how many articles, casenotes, or comments discussed a case in which the defendant's name was the Hubschman Construction Co.
   ANSWER:

7. State the name of the case from Question 6.
   ANSWER:

8. Using the Author/Title Index, provide the complete citation for a book review of Women Winning.
   ANSWER:

9. What grade did the Current Law Index assign the book in the review from Question 8?
   ANSWER:

10. Use the Table of Statutes. In what law review did an article, casenote, or comment discussing the Alberta Planning Act of 1977 appear? Abbreviate the title according to A Uniform System of Citation, 13th ed.
   ANSWER:

11. Using the Subject Index, provide the complete citation to an article on employers' liability which was published in the New Mexico Law Review.
   ANSWER:

12. Using only the 1979 bound volume of Shepard's Law Review Citations, state how many law review articles cited 79 Harvard Law Review 534.
   ANSWER:

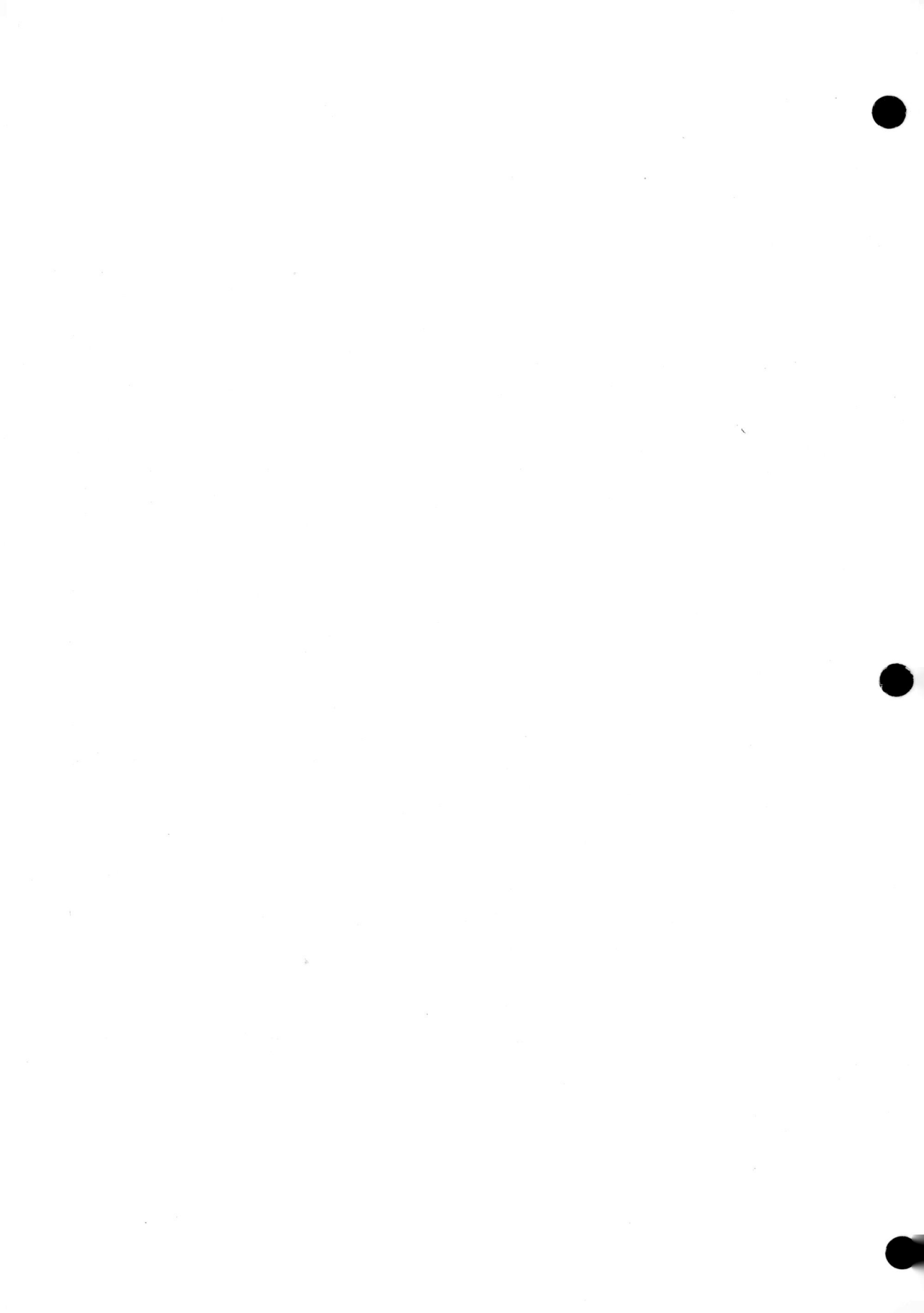

ASSIGNMENT XXI
LEGAL PERIODICAL INDEXES
EXERCISE D

GOALS: 1) To introduce you to the two leading legal periodical indexes.
2) To make you familiar with the differences in indexing formats, so that you will be able to use them effectively and without misinterpretation.
3) To give you practice at citing law review articles, comments, casenotes, and book reviews according to A Uniform System of Citation, 13th ed.
4) To show you how to find law review articles and cases which have cited a particular law review article.

NOTE: When you are asked to provide a complete citation, state all information according to A Uniform System of Citation, 13th ed., Rule 16, in the typeface style for briefs and memoranda. It will be necessary to examine the article itself before citing it, because there are often differences between the title of the article and the title listed in the index, and in order to tell whether a student has written the material.

To answer Questions 1-4, use Cumulation 18 of the Index to Legal Periodicals. Each question can be answered from an entry or entries in that volume.

1. Using the Subject and Author Index, provide the complete citation to an article on cooperatives published in the North Dakota Law Review.
   ANSWER:

2. Using the Subject and Author Index, list the titles of the articles written by Dan P. Danilov.
   ANSWER:

3. Using the Table of Cases, state how many articles, casenotes, or comments were written about Bounds v. Smith.
   ANSWER:

4. Using the Book Review Index, provide the complete citation for the review of a book by J. Goodfield, Playing God.
   ANSWER:

To answer Questions 5-11, use Volume 2 of the Current Law Index. Each question can be answered from an entry or entries in that volume.

5. Using the Author/Title Index, list the titles of the articles written by Christopher C. Joyner.
   ANSWER:

6. Using the Table of Cases, tell how many articles, casenotes, or comments discussed a case in which the defendant's name was the Gardner-Denver Co.
   ANSWER:

7. State the name of the case from Question 6.
   ANSWER:

8. Using the Author/Title Index, provide the complete citation for a book review of You Can Beat City Hall.
   ANSWER:

9. What grade did the Current Law Index assign the book in the review from Question 8?
   ANSWER:

10. Use the Table of Statutes. In what law review did an article, casenote, or comment discussing the Classified Information Procedures Act appear? Abbreviate the title according to A Uniform System of Citation, 13th ed.
    ANSWER:

11. Using the Subject Index, provide the complete citation to an article on indemnity against liability which was published in St. Mary's Law Journal.
    ANSWER:

12. Using only the 1979 bound volume of Shepard's Law Review Citations, state how many law review articles cited 1971 University of Illinois Law Forum 655.
    ANSWER:

INTRODUCTION
TO CHAPTER XXII
BRITISH LAW

The purpose of this exercise is to introduce you to some of the principal British legal publications. Even though our terminology may differ, there are basic similarities between British and American legal materials.

Questions 1-3 involve the use of Halsbury's Statutes of England, 3d ed. Halsbury's Statutes is an unofficial compilation of statutes, arranged by broad topic and accompanied by annotations and explanatory essays.

Question 4 involves the use of the English and Empire Digest to find case citations. The English and Empire Digest is simply a digest of Commonwealth case law, similar in format to American digests. As with American digests, the English and Empire Digest can be used to find the complete citation to a case if you know its name, or to retrieve points of law by subject.

To answer Question 5 you must use the citation form of A Uniform System of Citation, 13th ed., to cite the cases from Question 4. They are all in the English Reports, Full Reprint Series, the most complete collection of British cases from 1220 to 1865.

Question 6 requires you to try the subject approach with the English and Empire Digest using the indexes at the ends of the volumes.

Questions 7 and 8 introduce you to Halsbury's Laws of England, which is an encyclopedia of case and statutory law, and is generally similar to Corpus Juris Secundum or American Jurisprudence 2d but contains more coverage of statutory law.

Before beginning, read Chapter 19, "English and Canadian Materials," in Cohen and Berring, How to Find the Law, 8th ed.

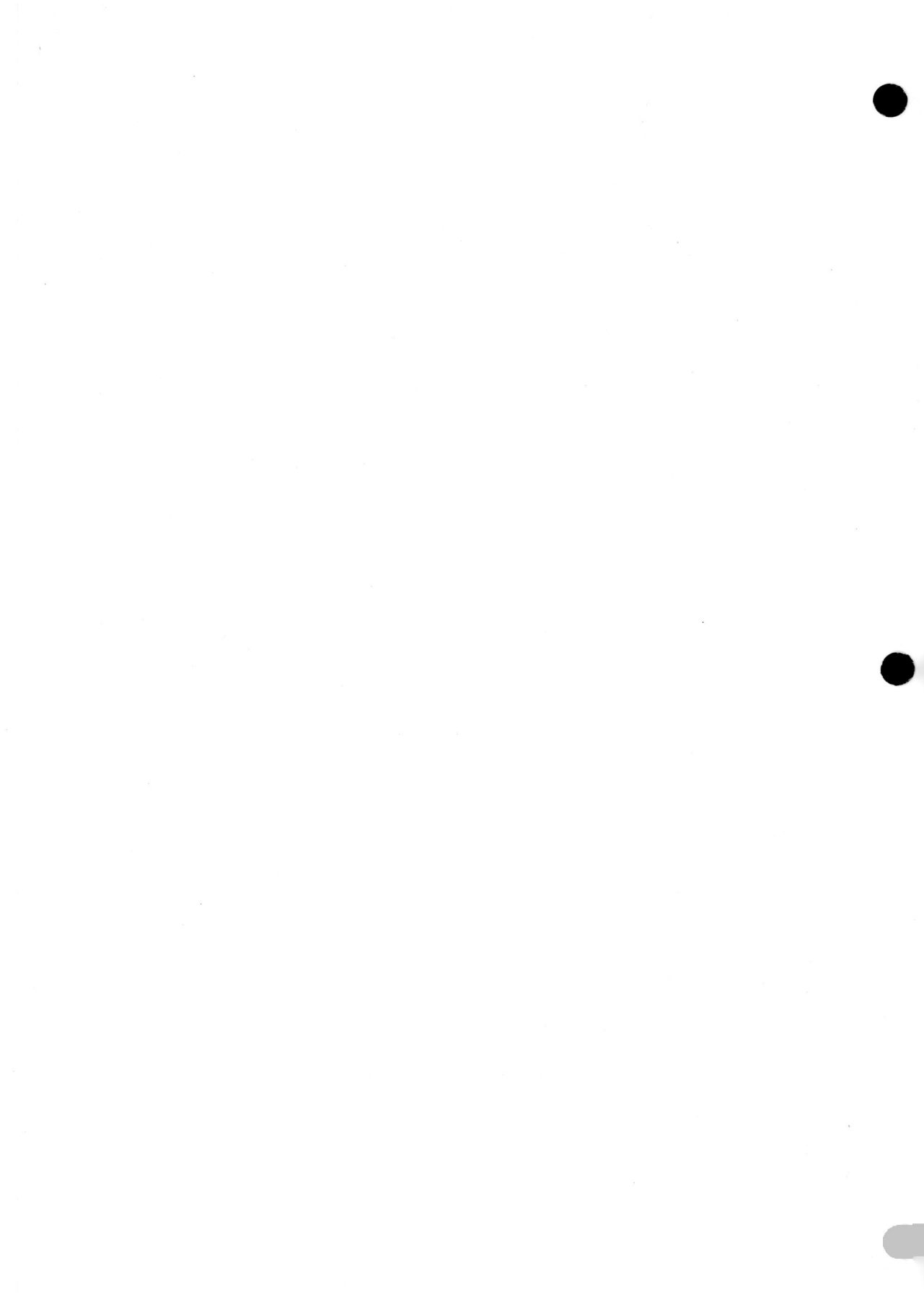

ASSIGNMENT XXII
BRITISH LAW
EXERCISE A

GOALS: 1) To acquaint you with key British legal publications which correspond to our digests, encyclopedias, and reporters.
2) To give you practice at finding British nominative court opinions.

STATUTORY LAW
To answer Questions 1-3 use <u>Halsbury's Statutes of England,</u> 3d ed. Begin with the volume titled "Tables of Statutes and Index for Vols. 1-50."

1. If a child is born to a woman who is a citizen of the United Kingdom, is the child automatically a citizen by descent?
   ANSWER:

2. Is the emission of dark smoke from a chimney an offense and if so who is the offender?
   ANSWER:

3. Using the appropriate table, list the name and year of the act whose citation is 56 Geo. 3, ch. 52.
   ANSWER:

CASE LAW
To answer Questions 4 and 6 use the <u>English and Empire Digest.</u>

4. Find the cases below where they are digested. List the year of the opinion, volume number, reporter name, and page number as the digest lists them. If there is more than one citation, list them all. NOTE: Finding cases in the <u>Digest</u> may be difficult since the blue-banded volumes are being replaced by green-banded volumes which contain different paging. Do the following:

   1) Find the case name in the blue-banded Table of Cases. You will be given a volume and page number, and the digest entry (do not confuse these with the case citations).

2) Find the volume. If it is blue–banded, simply look up the case.

3) If it is green–banded, use the Table of Cases in the front. Find the correct page or case number and look up the case. The citation will be listed there.

a. Alardes v. Cambel. (NOTE: This case has changed volumes in the new edition of the Digest. You will find it in the volume containing "Arbitration.")
ANSWER:

b. Cage v. Russel.
ANSWER:

c. Abson v. Fenton.
ANSWER:

5. As you can see, each case from Question 4 was reprinted in the English Reports, Full Reprint Series. Provide full citations for them, using A Uniform System of Citation, 13th ed., Rules 10.4(c) and (e) and pp. 186–89. If you find it necessary to look up the case, do so.

a. ANSWER:

b. ANSWER:

c. ANSWER:

6. Begin with the subject index at the end of green–banded vol. 3 of the English and Empire Digest. Is a barrister exempt from jury duty?
ANSWER:

CASE AND STATUTORY LAW
To answer Questions 7 and 8 use <u>Halsbury's Laws of England</u>, 4th ed.

7. Begin with the Index. What degree of care and diligence is required of a bailee where both bailee and bailor benefit from the bailment?
    ANSWER:

8. Begin with the Index. If evidence is wrongfully obtained, does that render it automatically inadmissible?
    ANSWER:

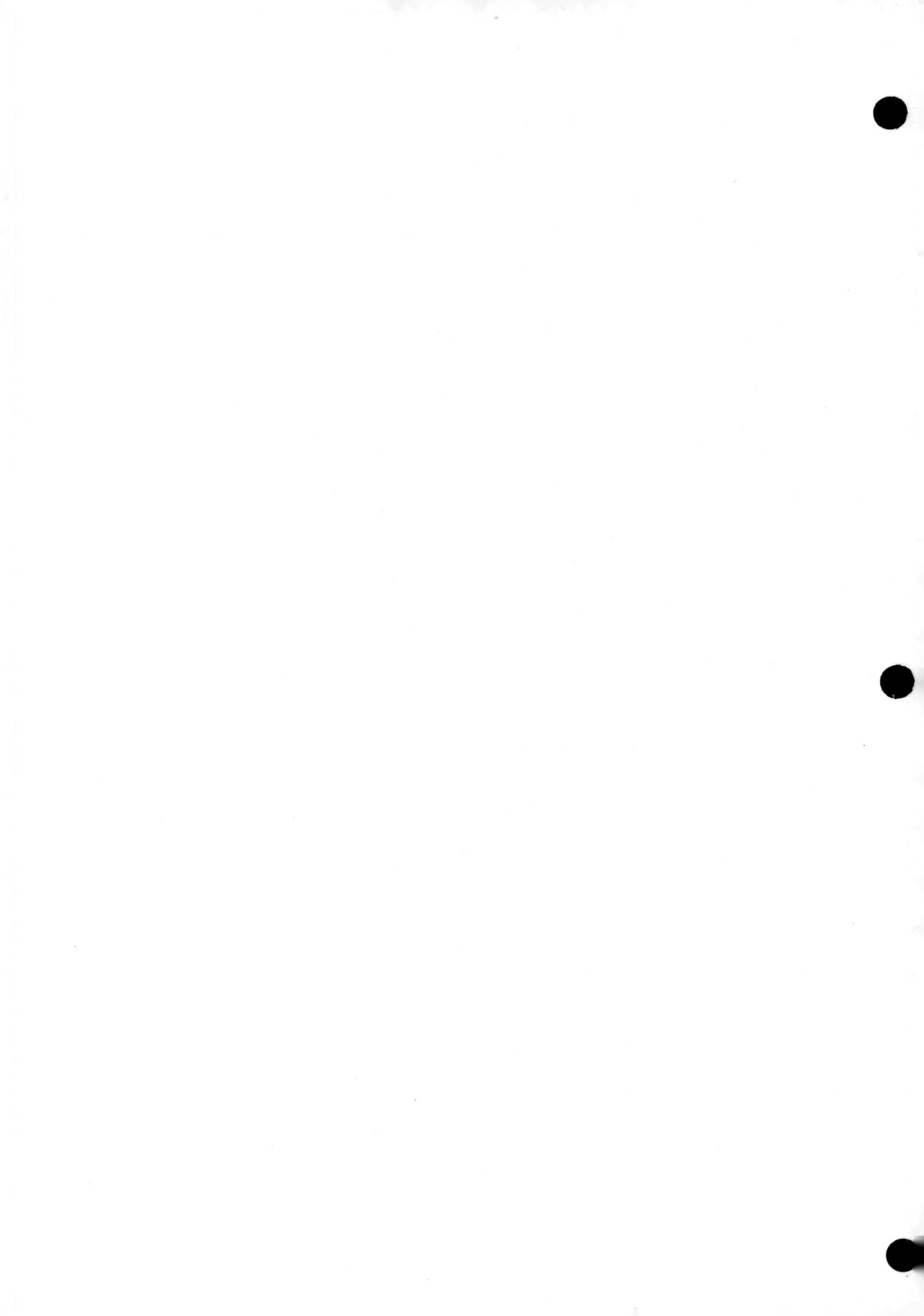

GOALS: 1) To acquaint you with key British legal publications which correspond to our digests, encyclopedias, and reporters.

  2) To give you practice at finding British nominative court opinions.

STATUTORY LAW

To answer Questions 1-3 use Halsbury's Statutes of England, 3d ed. Begin with the volume titled "Tables of Statutes and Index for Vols. 1-50."

1. In regards to an auction, who is a "puffer?"
    ANSWER:

2. May a sheriff temporarily act as a justice of the peace?
    ANSWER:

3. Using the appropriate table, list the name and year of the act whose citation is 27 Hen. 8, ch. 10.
    ANSWER:

CASE LAW

To answer Questions 4 and 6 use the English and Empire Digest.

4. Find the cases below where they are digested. List the year of the opinion, volume number, reporter name, and page number as the digest lists them. If there is more than one citation, list them all. NOTE: Finding cases in the Digest may be difficult since the blue-banded volumes are being replaced by green-banded volumes which contain different paging. Do the following:

    1) Find the case name in the blue-banded Table of Cases. You will be given a volume and page number, and the digest entry (do not confuse these with the case citations).

2) Find the volume. If it is blue-banded, simply look up the case.

3) If it is green-banded, use the Table of Cases in the front. Find the correct page or case number and look up the case. The citation will be listed there.

a. <u>Parker v. Gordon.</u>
   ANSWER:

b. <u>Parke v. Mears.</u>
   ANSWER:

c. <u>Jenkinson v. Allisson.</u>
   ANSWER:

5. As you can see, each case from Question 4 was reprinted in the <u>English Reports, Full Reprint Series.</u> Provide full citations for them, using <u>A Uniform System of Citation,</u> 13th ed., Rules 10.4(c) and (e) <u>and</u> pp. 186-8<u>9.</u> If you find it necessary to look up the case, do so.

a. **ANSWER:**

b. **ANSWER:**

c. **ANSWER:**

6. Begin with the subject index at the end of green-banded vol. 18 of the <u>English and Empire Digest.</u> Generally, is a landlord prohibited from making a distress for rent after sunset?
   ANSWER:

CASE AND STATUTORY LAW
To answer Questions 7 and 8 use <u>Halsbury's Laws of England</u>, 4th ed.

7. Begin with the Index. If a minor receives a gift of a legal estate of land, what actually vests in the minor?
    ANSWER:

8. Begin with the Index. May a barrister be sued by a client for negligence in respect to the barrister's management of a case?
    ANSWER:

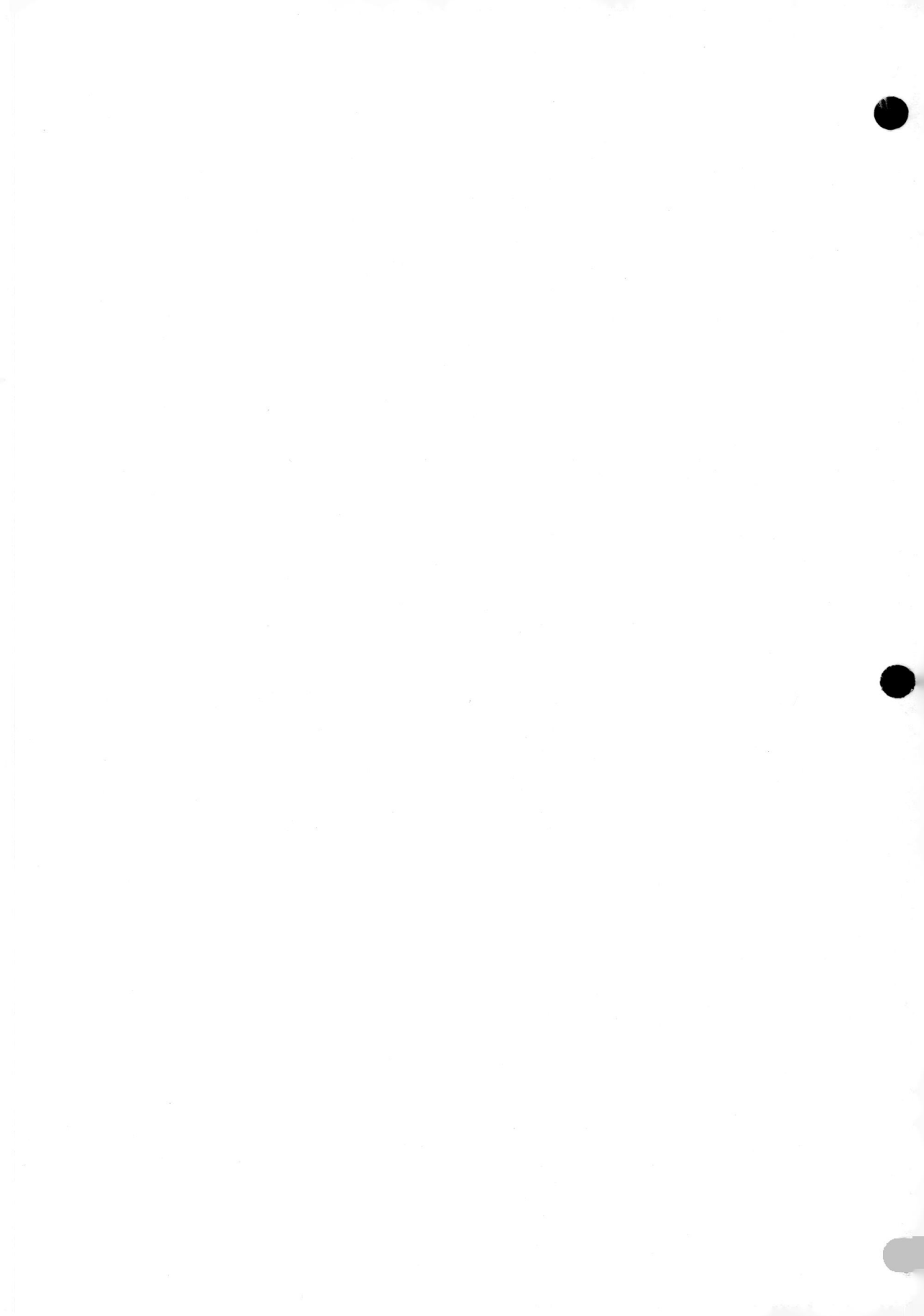

GOALS: 1) To acquaint you with key British legal publications which correspond
to our digests, encyclopedias, and reporters.
2) To give you practice at finding British nominative court opinions.

STATUTORY LAW

To answer Questions 1-3 use Halsbury's Statutes of England, 3d ed. Begin with
the volume titled "Tables of Statutes and Index for Vols. 1-50."

1. Does the transfer or assignment of a bill of sale need to be registered?
ANSWER:

2. What government official has jurisdiction over prisons?
ANSWER:

3. Using the appropriate table, list the name and year of the act whose
citation is 29 Car. 2, ch. 3.
ANSWER:

CASE LAW

To answer Questions 4 and 6 use the English and Empire Digest.

4. Find the cases below where they are digested. List the year of the opinion,
volume number, reporter name, and page number as the digest lists them.
If there is more than one citation, list them all. NOTE: Finding cases in
the Digest may be difficult since the blue-banded volumes are being replaced
by green-banded volumes which contain different paging. Do the following:

1) Find the case name in the blue-banded Table of Cases. You will be
given a volume and page number, and the digest entry (do not confuse
these with the case citations).

2) Find the volume. If it is blue-banded, simply look up the case.

3) If it is green-banded, use the Table of Cases in the front. Find the correct page or case number and look up the case. The citation will be listed there.

a. Winch v. Winch.
   ANSWER:

b. Yeates v. Groves.
   ANSWER:

c. Syred v. Carruthers.
   ANSWER:

5. As you can see, each case from Question 4 was reprinted in the English Reports, Full Reprint Series. Provide full citations for them, using A Uniform System of Citation, 13th ed., Rules 10.4(c) and (e) and pp. 186-89. If you find it necessary to look up the case, do so.

a. **ANSWER:**

b. **ANSWER:**

c. **ANSWER:**

6. Begin with the subject index at the end of green-banded vol. 13 of the English and Empire Digest. May the public attend a coroner's inquest?
   ANSWER:

CASE AND STATUTORY LAW
To answer Questions 7 and 8 use <u>Halsbury's Laws of England</u>, 4th ed.

7. Begin with the Index. What is the minimum age for gaming on licensed premises?
    ANSWER:

8. Begin with the Index. What sentences may be imposed on an offender regardless of the offender's age?
    ANSWER:

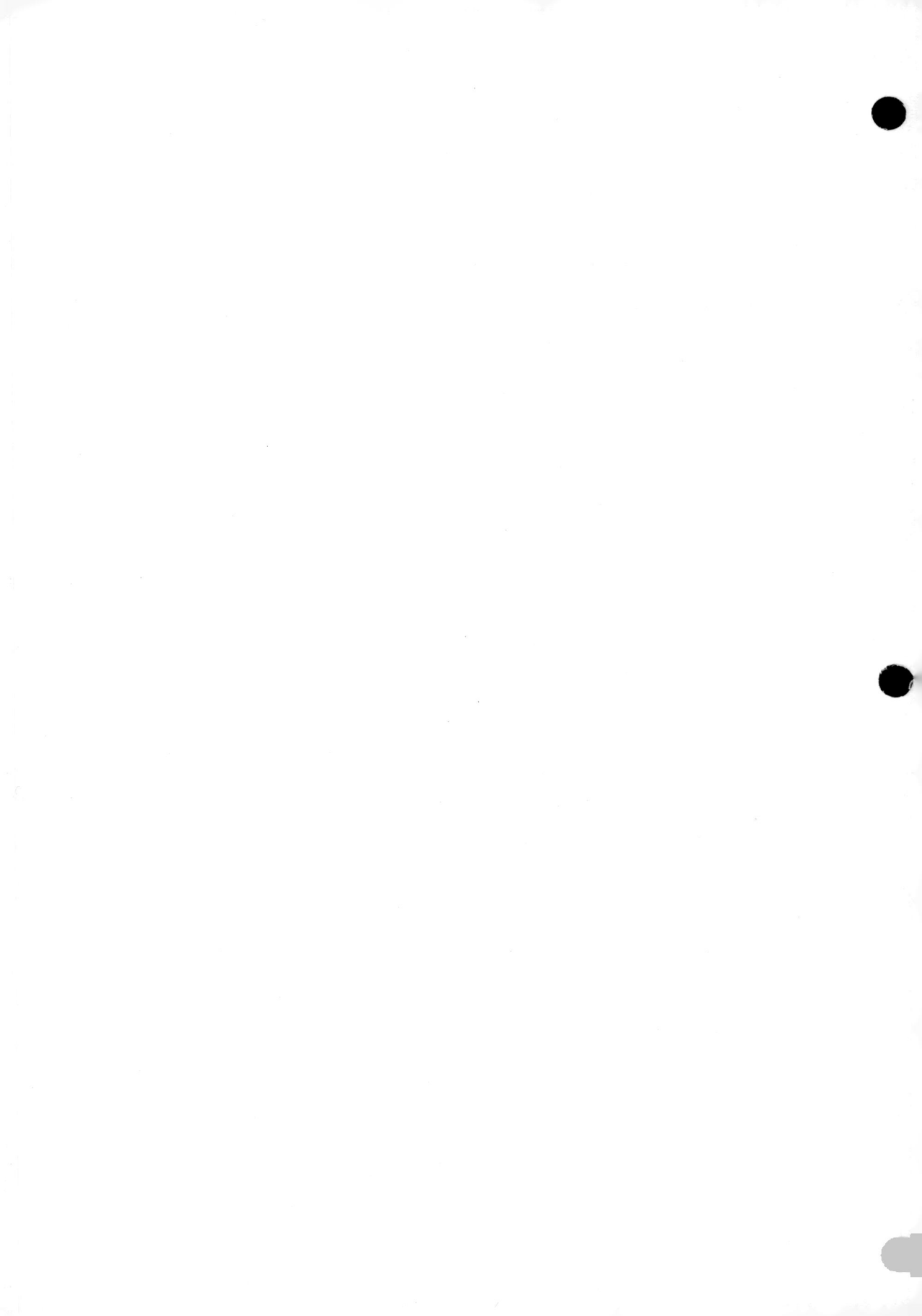

ASSIGNMENT XXII
BRITISH LAW
EXERCISE D

GOALS: 1)   To acquaint you with key British legal publications which correspond
to our digests, encyclopedias, and reporters.
2)   To give you practice at finding British nominative court opinions.

STATUTORY LAW
To answer Questions 1-3 use <u>Halsbury's Statutes of England</u>, 3d ed. Begin with
the volume titled "Tables of Statutes and Index for Vols. 1-50."

1.   Do coroners have the right to investigate when treasure trove is found?
ANSWER:

2.   Must limited partnerships be registered?
ANSWER:

3.   Using the appropriate table, list the name and year of the act whose
citation is 25 Geo. 2, ch. 36.
ANSWER:

CASE LAW
To answer Questions 4 and 6 use the <u>English and Empire Digest</u>.

4.   Find the cases below where they are digested. List the year of the opinion,
volume number, reporter name, and page number as the digest lists them.
If there is more than one citation, list them all. NOTE: Finding cases in
the <u>Digest</u> may be difficult since the blue-banded volumes are being replaced
by green-banded volumes which contain different paging. Do the following:

1)   Find the case name in the blue-banded Table of Cases. You will be
given a volume and page number, and the digest entry (do not confuse
these with the case citations).

2) Find the volume. If it is blue-banded, simply look up the case.

3) If it is green-banded, use the Table of Cases in the front. Find the correct page or case number and look up the case. The citation will be listed there.

a.   Briggs v. Calverly.
     ANSWER:

b.   Cumberland v. Planche.
     ANSWER:

c.   Attorney General v. Dimond.
     ANSWER:

5.   As you can see, each case from Question 4 was reprinted in the English Reports, Full Reprint Series. Provide full citations for them, using A Uniform System of Citation, 13th ed., Rules 10.4(c) and (e) and pp. 186-89. If you find it necessary to look up the case, do so.

a.   **ANSWER:**

b.   **ANSWER:**

c.   **ANSWER:**

6.   Begin with the subject index at the end of green-banded vol. 7 of the English and Empire Digest. Can parol evidence be used in a boundary dispute?
     ANSWER:

CASE AND STATUTORY LAW

To answer Questions 7 and 8 use <u>Halsbury's Laws of England</u>, 4th ed.

7. Begin with the Index. When does the period of copyright end for a sound recording published in 1969?
    ANSWER:

8. Begin with the Index. Is the fact that respondent has committed adultery sufficient to prove the irretrievable breakdown of marriage and therefore justify divorce?
    ANSWER:

INTRODUCTION
TO CHAPTER XXIII
WESTLAW

The following exercise will require you to practice some basic aspects of WESTLAW searching. You should know how to sign on, use the terminal, formulate a query, and perform basic operations on WESTLAW before you begin this assignment. We recommend that you keep a copy of the <u>WESTLAW Reference Manual</u> by your side as you work through the assignment.

Computerization is the most revolutionary development in legal research since the invention of key numbers almost a century ago. Chances are that during your career as an attorney you will use WESTLAW, LEXIS, or both. We recommend that you use your law school's legal research data bases as much as you can, since only through practice will you acquire skill.

Before beginning these problems, read about WESTLAW in Chapter 22 of Cohen and Berring, <u>How to Find the Law,</u> 8th ed.

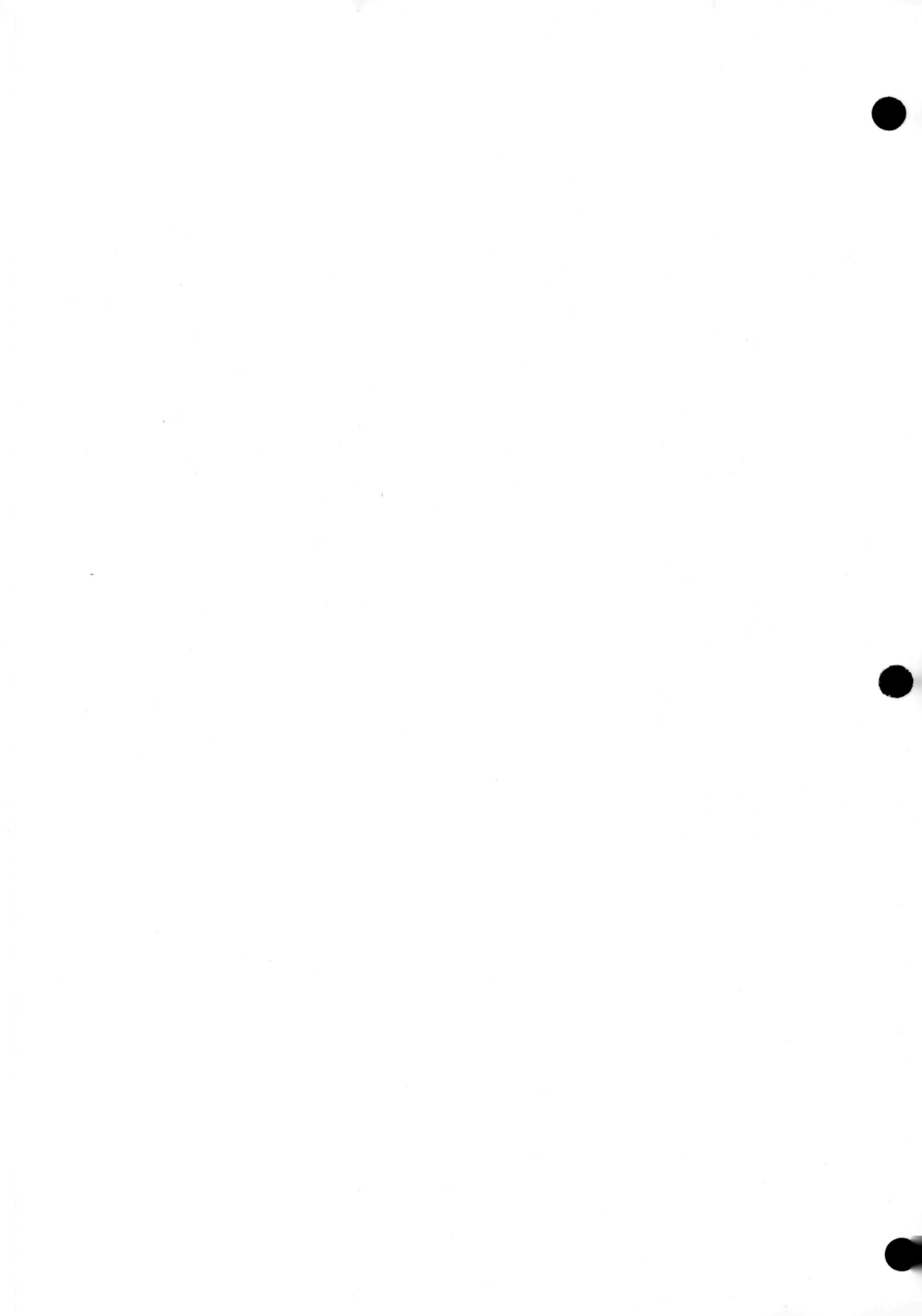

ASSIGNMENT XXIII
WESTLAW
EXERCISE A

GOALS: 1) To give you practice at formulating effective search strategies.
2) To introduce you to field searching.
3) To give you practice at using WESTLAW as a citator for cases and statutes.
4) To give you practice at using Black's Law Dictionary and Shepard's on WESTLAW.
5) To introduce you to key number searching on WESTLAW.

1. Find the 1981 Illinois Supreme Court case which adopted comparative negligence as the law in Illinois. What are the name and regional citation of the case?
   ANSWER:

2. How many WESTLAW screens long is the full text of the case from Question 1?
   ANSWER:

3. Use WESTLAW as a citator for the case from Question 1 and tell how many Illinois court opinions decided prior to 1983 cited its regional citation.
   ANSWER:

4. Shepardize the opinion from Question 1 on WESTLAW. What is the regional citation of the citing New Hampshire case?
   ANSWER:

5. Use Black's Law Dictionary on WESTLAW and state the definition of "curagulos."
   ANSWER:

6. How many majority opinions did Judge Rooney of the Wyoming Supreme Court write before 1982?
ANSWER:

7. Before 1982, Judge Rooney of Question 6 wrote a dissent in a case involving a holographic will. What are the name, regional citation, and year of the case?
ANSWER:

8. Find a First Circuit U.S. Court of Appeals case decided prior to 1980 that cited 15 U.S.C. § 1801, concerning newspapers. What are the name and docket number of the case?
ANSWER:

9. Assume that you are seeking the C.F.R. provision restricting the sale of government small arms weapons and ammunition to members of the National Rifle Association. Cite the title and part.
ANSWER:

10. Find the Topic Outline at the beginning of the topic "Products Liability" in West's Ninth Decennial Digest.

   a. Which key number covers product design in general?
   ANSWER:

   b. Use WESTLAW and tell how many cases decided before 1983 published in the Atlantic Reporter contain the topic and key number from the previous question and concern lawn mowers as the product at issue.
   ANSWER:

ASSIGNMENT XXIII
WESTLAW
EXERCISE B

GOALS: 1) To give you practice at formulating effective search strategies.
        2) To introduce you to field searching.
        3) To give you practice at using WESTLAW as a citator for cases
            and statutes.
        4) To give you practice at using Black's Law Dictionary and Shepard's
            on WESTLAW.
        5) To introduce you to key number searching on WESTLAW.

1. Find the 1975 Alaska Supreme Court case which adopted comparative
    negligence as the law in Alaska. What are the name and regional citation
    of the case?
    ANSWER:

2. How many WESTLAW screens long is the full text of the case from Question
    1?
    ANSWER:

3. Use WESTLAW as a citator for the case from Question 1 and tell how many
    Alaska court opinions decided prior to 1983 cited its regional citation.
    ANSWER:

4. Shepardize the opinion from Question 1 on WESTLAW. What is the regional
    citation of the Wyoming decision which cites headnote 25 of the cited case?
    ANSWER:

5. Use Black's Law Dictionary on WESTLAW and state the definition of "doun."
    ANSWER:

303

6. How many majority opinions did Judge Liacos of the Massachusetts Supreme Judicial Court write before 1982?
   ANSWER:

7. Before 1982, Judge Liacos of Question 6 wrote a dissent in a case involving attorneys' fees in a tax case. What are the name, regional citation, and year of the case?
   ANSWER:

8. Find a First Circuit U.S. Court of Appeals case decided prior to 1982 that cited 17 U.S.C. § 503, concerning copyright infringement. What are the name and docket number of the case?
   ANSWER:

9. According to the C.F.R., what is the maximum noise level for mopeds manufactured after January 1, 1983?
   ANSWER:

10. Find the Topic Outline at the beginning of the topic, "Products Liability in West's <u>Ninth Decennial Digest</u>.

    a. Which key number covers product design in general?
       ANSWER:

    b. Use WESTLAW and tell how many cases decided before 1983 published in the <u>North Eastern Reporter</u> contain the topic and key number from the previous question and concern lawn mowers as the product at issue.
       ANSWER:

ASSIGNMENT XXIII
WESTLAW
EXERCISE C

GOALS: 1) To give you practice at formulating effective search strategies.
2) To introduce you to field searching.
3) To give you practice at using WESTLAW as a citator for cases and statutes.
4) To give you practice at using Black's Law Dictionary and Shepard's on WESTLAW.
5) To introduce you to key number searching on WESTLAW.

1. Find the 1973 Florida Supreme Court case which adopted comparative negligence as the law in Florida. What are the name and regional citation of the case?
ANSWER:

2. How many WESTLAW screens long is the full text of the case from Question 1?
ANSWER:

3. Use WESTLAW as a citator for the case from Question 1 and tell how many Florida court opinions decided prior to 1975 cited its regional citation.
ANSWER:

4. Shepardize the opinion from Question 1 on WESTLAW. What is the regional citation of the citing Tennessee case?
ANSWER:

5. Use Black's Law Dictionary on WESTLAW and state the definition of "finem facere."
ANSWER:

6. How many majority opinions did Judge Birdsong of the Georgia Court of Appeals write before 1982?
   ANSWER:

7. Before 1982, Judge Birdsong of Question 6 wrote a dissent in a case involving workers' compensation suits by both the second wife and third wife of the decedent. What are the name, regional citation, and year of the case?
   ANSWER:

8. Find a Tenth Circuit U.S. Court of Appeals case decided prior to 1982 that cited 43 U.S.C. § 1334, concerning the leasing of the Continental Shelf. What are the name and docket number of the case?
   ANSWER:

9. Cite the C.F.R. provision which forbids bicycle riding at the National Capital Airports.
   ANSWER:

10. Find the Topic Outline at the beginning of the topic "Products Liability" in West's <u>Ninth Decennial Digest</u>.

    a. Which key number covers product design in general?
       ANSWER:

    b. Use WESTLAW and tell how many cases decided before 1983 published in the <u>Southern Reporter</u> contain the topic and key number from the previous question and concern lawn mowers as the product at issue.
       ANSWER:

ASSIGNMENT XXIII
WESTLAW
EXERCISE D

GOALS: 1) To give you practice at formulating effective search strategies.
2) To introduce you to field searching.
3) To give you practice at using WESTLAW as a citator for cases and statutes.
4) To give you practice at using Black's Law Dictionary and Shepard's on WESTLAW.
5) To introduce you to key number searching on WESTLAW.

1. Find the 1979 Michigan Supreme Court case which adopted comparative negligence as the law in Michigan. What are the name and regional citation of the case?
    ANSWER:

2. How many WESTLAW screens long is the full text of the case from Question 1?
    ANSWER:

3. Use WESTLAW as a citator for the case from Question 1 and tell how many Michigan court opinions decided prior to 1981 cited its regional citation.
    ANSWER:

4. Shepardize the opinion from Question 1 on WESTLAW. What is the regional citation of the Iowa decision which cites headnote 8 of the cited case?
    ANSWER:

5. Use Black's Law Dictionary on WESTLAW and state the definition of "mensa et thoro."
    ANSWER:

6. How many majority opinions did Judge Exum of the North Carolina Supreme Court write before 1982?
    ANSWER:

7. Before 1982, Judge Exum of Question 6 wrote a dissent in a case involving the defendant's rape of his niece. What are the name, regional citation, and year of the case?
    ANSWER:

8. Find a Seventh Circuit U.S. Court of Appeals case decided prior to 1983 but after 1970 that cited 25 U.S.C. § 331, the General Allotment Act. What are the name and docket number of the case?
    ANSWER:

9. According to the C.F.R., how much of a ketchup container should be filled with ketchup?
    ANSWER:

10. Find the Topic Outline at the beginning of the topic "Products Liability" in West's Ninth Decennial Digest.

    a. Which key number covers product warnings or instructions in general?
        ANSWER:

    b. Use WESTLAW and tell how many cases decided before 1983 published in the Pacific Reporter contain the topic and key number from the previous question and concern lawn mowers as the product at issue.
        ANSWER:

INTRODUCTION
TO CHAPTER XXIV
LEXIS

These problems assume that you are familiar with basic LEXIS use. Before beginning this exercise, you should know how to sign on to LEXIS, change libraries and files, and formulate searches using connectors and segments. If you have not attained this level of proficiency, ask your instructor to help you. We recommend that you read the LEXIS Handbook and have it with you while you work these problems. We also recommend that you use LEXIS whenever possible while you are a law student, since you will only develop LEXIS skill through practice.

Some of these problems require the same type of search that you used on WESTLAW. Thus, if you have completed both problem sets you might want to copy your search strategies on each and save them in order to contrast query formulation on LEXIS and WESTLAW.

Before beginning these problems, read about LEXIS in Chapter 22 of Cohen and Berring, How to Find the Law, 8th ed.

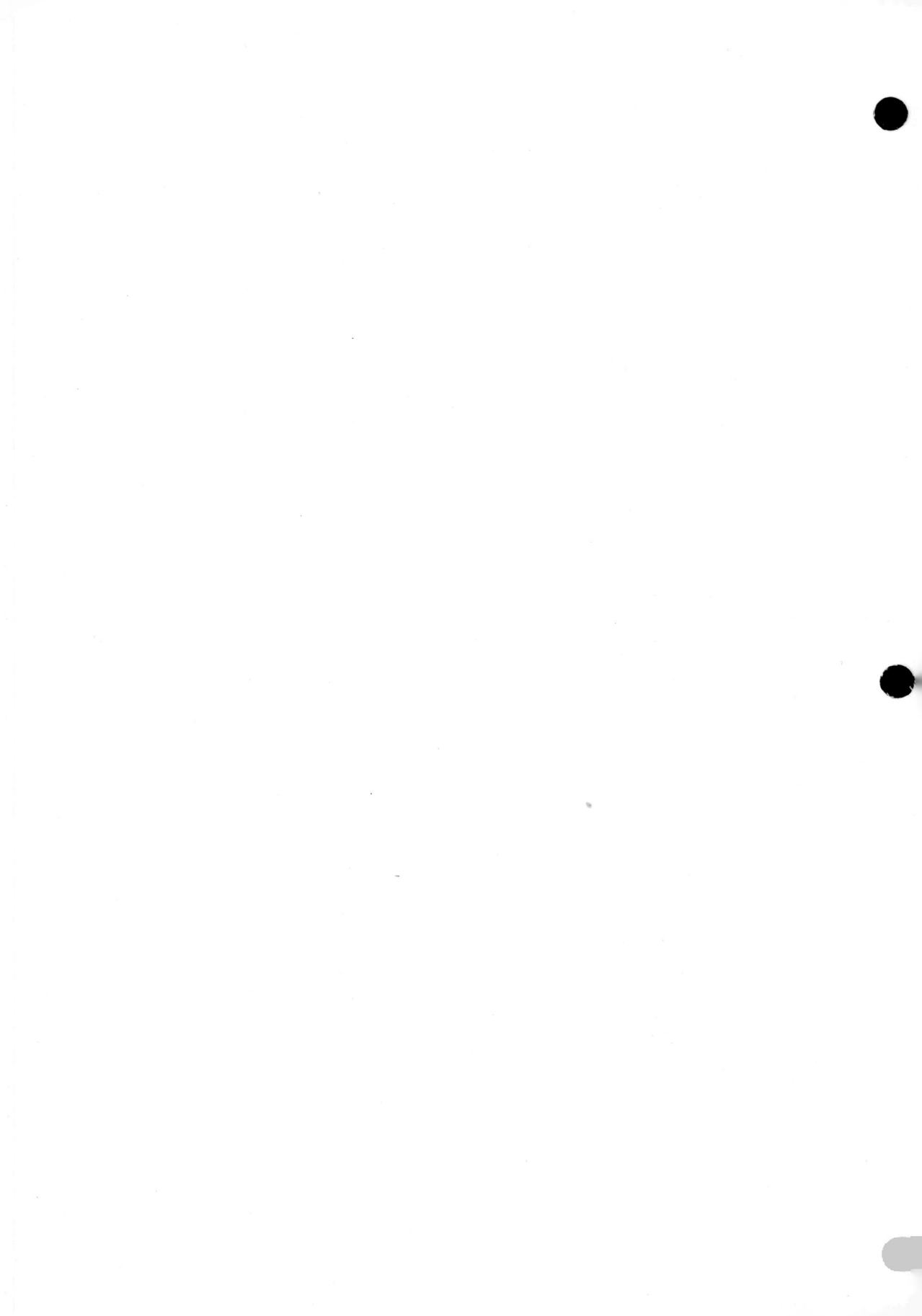

ASSIGNMENT XXIV
LEXIS
EXERCISE A

GOALS: 1) To give you practice at formulating effective search strategies.
         2) To introduce you to segment searching.
         3) To give you practice at using LEXIS as a citator for cases and statutes.
         4) To give you practice at using Auto-Cite.

1. Find the 1981 Illinois Supreme Court opinion which adopted comparative negligence as the law in Illinois. What are the name and official citation of the opinion? NOTE: When choosing libraries, view more than the first screen of libraries. Do not use the STATES library.
    ANSWER:

2. How many LEXIS screens long is the full text of the case from Question 1?
    ANSWER:

3. How many Illinois court opinions decided prior to 1983 cited the case from Question 1?
    ANSWER:

4. Assume that you are seeking an opinion whose name is Dinkins v. Kinney. You know it is a state case but do not know which state. What are the official citation and date?
    ANSWER:

5. Using Auto-Cite, state the unofficial citation for the case from Question 4 (the Auto-Cite key is in the upper left-hand corner of the keyboard).
    ANSWER:

311

6. How many opinions (including dissents and concurrences) did Judge Rooney of the Wyoming Supreme Court write before 1982?
   ANSWER:

7. Before 1982, Judge Rooney of Question 6 wrote a dissent to an opinion involving a holographic will. What is the name of the case?
   ANSWER:

8. Find a First Circuit U.S. Court of Appeals case decided prior to 1980 that cited 15 U.S.C. § 1801, which concerns newspapers. What are the name and citation of the case?
   ANSWER:

9. Assume that you are seeking the C.F.R. provision restricting the sale of government small arms weapons and ammunition to members of the National Rifle Association. Cite the title and part.
   ANSWER:

10. Assume that you are seeking some guidance as to whether appellate counsel has an obligation to inform a client of his or her right to a malpractice suit against trial counsel. Use the ABA library and state the date, number, title, etc. of the opinion or code section that answers this question most directly.
    ANSWER:

ASSIGNMENT XXIV
LEXIS
EXERCISE B

GOALS: 1) To give you practice at formulating effective search strategies.
2) To introduce you to segment searching.
3) To give you practice at using LEXIS as a citator for cases and statutes.
4) To give you practice at using Auto-Cite.

1. Find the 1975 Alaska Supreme Court opinion which adopted comparative negligence as the law in Alaska. What are the name and official citation of the opinion? NOTE: When choosing libraries, view more than the first screen of libraries. Do not use the STATES library.
ANSWER:

2. How many LEXIS screens long is the full text of the case from Question 1?
ANSWER:.

3. How many Alaska court opinions decided prior to 1983 cited the case from Question 1?
ANSWER:

4. Assume that you are seeking an opinion whose name is Williams v. Slusser. You know it is a state case but do not know which state. What are the official citation and date?
ANSWER:

5. Using Auto-Cite, state the citation of the A.L.R.3d annotation which cites the case from Question 4 (the Auto-Cite key is in the upper left-hand corner of the keyboard).
ANSWER:

6. How many opinions (including dissents and concurrences) did Judge Liacos of the Massachusetts Supreme Judicial Court write before 1982?
ANSWER:

7. Before 1982, Judge Liacos of Question 6 wrote a dissent to an opinion involving attorneys' fees in a tax case. What is the name of the case?
ANSWER:

8. Find a First Circuit U.S. Court of Appeals case decided prior to 1982 that cited 17 U.S.C. § 503, concerning copyright infringement. What are the name and citation of the case?
ANSWER:

9. According to the C.F.R., what is the maximum noise level for mopeds manufactured after January 1, 1983?
ANSWER:

10. Assume that you are seeking guidance as to whether a husband and wife who are both lawyers may represent different interests or associate with firms representing different interests. Use the ABA library and state the date, number, title, etc. of the opinion or code section that answers this question most directly.
ANSWER:

ASSIGNMENT XXIV
LEXIS
EXERCISE C

GOALS: 1) To give you practice at formulating effective search strategies.
2) To introduce you to segment searching.
3) To give you practice at using LEXIS as a citator for cases and statutes.
4) To give you practice at using Auto-Cite.

1. Find the 1973 Florida Supreme Court opinion which adopted comparative negligence as the law in Florida. What are the name and official citation of the opinion? NOTE: When choosing libraries, view more than the first screen of libraries. Do not use the STATES library.
ANSWER:

2. How many LEXIS screens long is the full text of the case from Question 1?
ANSWER:

3. How many Florida court opinions decided prior to 1975 cited the case from Question 1?
ANSWER:

4. Assume that you are seeking an opinion whose name is <u>Berring v. Jacob</u>. You know it is a state case but do not know which state. What are the official citation and date?
ANSWER:

5. Using Auto-Cite, state the citation of the A.L.R.2d annotation which cites the case from Question 4 (the Auto-Cite key is in the upper left-hand corner of the keyboard).
ANSWER:

6. How many opinions (including dissents and concurrences) did Judge Birdsong of the Georgia Court of Appeals write before 1982?
   ANSWER:

7. Before 1982, Judge Birdsong of Question 6 wrote a dissent to an opinion involving medical malpractice, wrongful death, and a statute of limitations. What is the name of the case?
   ANSWER:

8. Find a Tenth Circuit U.S. Court of Appeals case decided prior to 1982 that cited 43 U.S.C. § 1334, concerning the leasing of the Continental Shelf. What are the name and citation of the case?
   ANSWER:

9. Cite the C.F.R. provision which forbids bicycle riding at the National Capital Airports.
   ANSWER:

10. Assume that you are seeking guidance as to whether a former client of yours may mention you and include your photograph in a book she is writing. Use the ABA library and state the date, number, title, etc. of the opinion or code section that answers this question most directly.
    ANSWER:

ASSIGNMENT XXIV
LEXIS
EXERCISE D

GOALS: 1) To give you practice at formulating effective search strategies.
        2) To introduce you to segment searching.
        3) To give you practice at using LEXIS as a citator for cases and statutes.
        4) To give you practice at using Auto-Cite.

1.   Find the 1979 Michigan Supreme Court opinion which adopted comparative negligence as the law in Michigan. What are the name and official citation of the opinion? NOTE: When choosing libraries, view more than the first screen of libraries. Do not use the STATES library.
ANSWER:

2.   How many LEXIS screens long is the full text of the case from Question 1?
ANSWER:

3.   How many Michigan court opinions decided prior to 1981 cited the case from Question 1?
ANSWER:

4.   Assume that you are seeking an opinion whose name is <u>Yancy v. Gambee.</u> You know it is a state case but do not know which state. What are the official citation and date?
ANSWER:

5.   Using Auto-Cite, state the unofficial citation for the case from Question 4 (the Auto-Cite key is in the upper left-hand corner of the keyboard).
ANSWER:

6. How many opinions (including dissents and concurrences) did Judge Exum
    of the North Carolina Supreme Court write before 1982?
    ANSWER:

7. Before 1982, Judge Exum of Question 6 wrote a dissent to an opinion
    involving the defendant's rape of his niece. What is the name of the case?
    ANSWER:

8. Find a Seventh Circuit U.S. Court of Appeals case decided prior to 1975
    that cited 25 U.S.C. § 331, the General Allotment Act. What are the name
    and citation of the case?
    ANSWER:

9. According to the C.F.R., how much of a ketchup container should be filled
    with ketchup?
    ANSWER:

10. Assume that you are seeking guidance as to whether you may compensate
    your office administrator (who is not a lawyer) with a fixed annual salary
    plus a percentage of net profits. Use the ABA library and state the date,
    number, title, etc. of the opinion or code section that answers this question
    most directly.
    ANSWER:

†

Notes

Notes

Notes

Notes

Notes

Notes

Notes

Notes

Notes

Notes

Notes

Notes